D0569834

Community College Student Success

American Council on Education Series on Community Colleges
Series Editor: Richard Alfred

Titles in the Series

First in the World: Community Colleges and America's Future, by J. Noah Brown
Re-visioning Community Colleges, by Debbie Sydow and Richard Alfred
Student Success: From the Boardrooms to Classrooms, by Vanessa Smith Morest

Community College Student Success

From Boardrooms to Classrooms

Vanessa Smith Morest

Published in Partnership with
 American
Council on
Education™

Leadership and Advocacy

ROWMAN & LITTLEFIELD PUBLISHERS, INC.
Lanham • Boulder • New York • Toronto • Plymouth, UK

Published by Rowman & Littlefield Education
A division of Rowman & Littlefield Publishers, Inc.
A wholly owned subsidiary of The Rowman & Littlefield Publishing Group, Inc.
4501 Forbes Boulevard, Suite 200, Lanham, Maryland 20706
www.rowman.com

10 Thornbury Road, Plymouth PL6 7PP, United Kingdom

British Library Cataloguing in Publication Information Available

Library of Congress Cataloging-in-Publication Data

Morest, Vanessa Smith, 1969- author.
Student success : from boardrooms to classrooms / Vanessa Smith Morest.
p. cm. -- (The Community College Series)
Includes bibliographical references and index.
ISBN 978-1-4422-1480-4 (cloth : alk. paper) -- ISBN 978-1-4422-1482-8 (electronic)
1. Community colleges--United States. I. Title.
LB2328.M587 2012
378.1'5430973--dc23
2012045614

The paper used in this publication meets the minimum requirements of American National
Standard for Information Sciences Permanence of Paper for Printed Library Materials,
ANSI/NISO Z39.48-1992.

Printed in the United States of America

For my sons
Henry and Freddy Morest

Contents

Acknowledgments

The thought and research underlying this book are the direct result of opportunities to learn about community colleges given to me by others. First and foremost, I would like to thank Richard Alfred, Emeritus Professor of Higher Education at the University of Michigan, for inviting me to write this book for the Community College Series. I am indebted to him not only for providing the opportunity to bring my thoughts about student success together in a book, but also for his feedback and encouragement throughout the writing process. Appreciation is also extended to Patricia Carter, Executive Director of the Center for Community College Development, for her work in reviewing early drafts of the book and providing editorial suggestions.

From Board Rooms to Classrooms was inspired by the experience of working first as a researcher and then as a college administrator. I would like to thank Thomas Bailey, Director of the Community College Research Center (CCRC) at Columbia University, for his mentorship and for giving me the chance to become deeply involved in research on community colleges. The work of the CCRC and the National Center for Postsecondary Education are cited throughout this book as they have been pivotal to strengthening and expanding research on student success. Through the work of these Centers, Tom created a space for researchers and practitioners to come together as colleagues working toward a common goal to improve community colleges.

I would also like to thank David Levinson, President of Norwalk Community College for his mentorship and support. In 2007, I began working as a community college administrator and was fortunate to be entrusted with a role which allows me to have an institution-wide perspective and given the opportunity to build a department. As a result of this leadership opportunity, I have learned a great deal about the challenges of translating research into action. The faculty and staff of Norwalk Community College inspire me daily through their commitment to improving the lives of students.

I am also grateful for the support of colleagues and friends who have helped me to expand and develop my work as a researcher and practitioner. These include the scholars and staff associated with CCRC who made it possible for me to remain engaged with the Center after assuming my current position. In particular, Kevin Dougherty helped me think through many parts of this book by way of ongoing dialog and exchange of ideas. Many individuals have helped me better understand community college leadership. I would like to acknowledge in particular Jim Jacobs, Ted Wright, and Jacquee Belcher who have helped me to further my understanding of the organizational dynamics of community colleges.

Finally, writing a book takes time and attention away from important parts of life. I could not have devoted time to this project without the support and encouragement of my husband, Claude Morest, my children, Henry and Freddy Morest, and my mother, Sheila Smith.

Vanessa Smith Morest

July 28, 2012

The Community College Series

Community colleges currently enroll 7.2 million students in 1,200 institutions—one out of every two first-time students entering college and slightly less than one-half of all undergraduate students in the nation. By 2016, they are projected to enroll 7.5 million students, many of whom will be minority, lower income, and underprepared for work and further education. Community colleges are the fastest growing segment of higher education both in number of institutions and enrollment. Yet, remarkably, they are the least understood of postsecondary institutions in terms of literature and research describing their mission and role, organization and operations, and performance. This void invites quality scholarship on a segment of higher education in which interest is high and audiences are both substantial and growing. There is much in the higher education news about community colleges, but not the critical scholarship and analysis necessary to support and sustain dialogue about issues and challenges facing them.

The Community College Series is designed to produce and deliver books on current and emerging "hot topics" in community colleges, developed from a leader and managerial point of view. Our goal is to develop distinctive books on salient topics. Each book is expected to be practical and concise, provocative and engaging, and address multiple dimensions of a topic. Most books are written by a single author—a college executive who brings expert and practical understanding to a topic; an academic or researcher who has a unique slant and bank of information to bring to a topic; a policy analyst or agency official who possesses critical insights into an issue; a think tank scholar who has the capacity to identify and examine a challenge or issue that is likely to confront community colleges in the future. To ensure practicality and different viewpoints, authors are expected to solicit and present ideas from a variety of perspectives and to include examples or case studies on how institutions and leaders might deal with the topic from a strategic and operational perspective. Finally, to ensure that each book brings maximum value to the reading audience, authors are expected to present original research and employ out-of-the box thinking in manuscript development. Each book is expected to represent the very best thought on a topic at the time of publication.

Richard Alfred
Editor
Community College Series

Foreword

The landscape of community college reform and community college research has changed dramatically in the last 15 years. In the middle of the 1990s, a fundamental community college mission was to provide broad access to higher education. While there were a handful of scholars who studied community colleges, most research in higher education was still focused on the elite selective colleges. Community colleges did not receive anywhere near the scholarly attention commensurate either with their share of college students or with the importance of the problems and issues that confronted them. The institutional research function within community colleges was only rudimentary and rarely carried out analytic research focused on the role or performance of the institutions. And the most important educational reform movements of the last quarter of the 20th century almost completely ignored community colleges.

In contrast, in 2012, community colleges are at the center of the discussion of educational reform in Washington, DC, as well as in most state capitals, and they are the focus of major reform initiatives funded generously by private foundations. Scholarly research on the colleges has grown rapidly over the last decade, and many colleges and state community college systems have strengthened their internal research capacity. As a result, we have made great progress in our understanding of the problems confronting community colleges, the nature of their institutional performance, and the effectiveness of reform strategies.

This growing knowledge base is evident in Vanessa Smith Morest's timely and insightful book, *Student Success: From Board Rooms to Classrooms*. It is worth noting that in addition to reporting on this new knowledge, Dr. Morest has participated in these developments. After completing her PhD in the sociology of education at Teachers College (TC), she worked as a research associate at TC's Community College Research Center (CCRC) for several years before becoming the Dean of Institutional Effectiveness at Norwalk Community College in Norwalk, Connecticut. At CCRC, she was a full-time scholarly investigator contributing to research on workforce development, transfer, STEM education, institutional research, the community college academic mission, and organizational change, among other areas. She also coedited CCRC's book, *Defending the Community College Equity Agenda.* Since 2006, she has overseen research from the inside, as an administrator with responsibilities within a functioning college. Dr. Morest thus brings a researcher's perspective leavened with knowledge of the realities of the day-to-day challenges of community college life. This experience results in a book that is both solidly grounded in rigorous research and useful and accessible to practitioners.

Community colleges have provided access to higher education for millions of low-income, first generation, immigrant, and minority students. The admissions requirements, registration procedures, tuition levels, location, class hours, and other factors were all designed to open the door to college to a wide variety of students. A look at the characteristics of community college students, especially when contrasted with those of students at four-year colleges, suggests that the colleges have made a great deal of progress in achieving their access mission. But during the last 15 years, policy makers, education reformers, and the faculty and administrators at the colleges themselves have all concluded that while access is crucial and while colleges must continue to pursue that mission, an increased focus on student outcomes is necessary. Although Dr. Morest ably demonstrates that published graduation rates distort the reality of community college student outcomes, it is still true that only a minority of community college students ever earns a credential. This number is too low. Ironically, some of the policies designed to promote access, such as permissive registration policies, can also make it more difficult for students to complete college. For example, very few students who register late have successful outcomes.

What are the barriers to student success at community colleges? While community colleges have fewer resources per student than colleges in other sectors of higher education, community colleges students tend to arrive with the more serious challenges to a positive college experience than students in four-year colleges. Dr. Morest divides these barriers into three areas—academic, social, and financial.

Most community college students arrive with weak academic skills. As a result, colleges provide developmental education or remedial services to help students catch up. But recent research has shown that these services are not effective, and many colleges and states are experimenting with policies and reforms designed to help these struggling students. These developments are nicely summarized in the book. While some of these reforms have promise,

Dr. Morest emphasizes the need for greater coordination and cooperation between community colleges and high schools.

One of the most widely accepted conclusions in higher education practice is that students have a better chance of success in college if they are engaged both academically and socially in the college. But because community colleges function as commuter schools with a predominantly part-time student body, it is extremely difficult to foster strong social and emotional student connections on the community college campus. Moreover, not only are most of the students part-time, but so too are many (and in some colleges, most) of the faculty. The lack of student engagement and connection to the colleges is a very difficult problem to solve. Learning communities and student success courses for first-year students can make some inroads. Much of the solution will have to be found in the classroom itself since that is in many cases the only place of serious contact between the colleges and the students. But community college classroom practice has received little attention—more on this below.

The third problem is financial. Community college students often have meager resources yet significant financial responsibilities; the majority work. Certainly financial aid is important, and research is beginning to show that simplification of financial aid application processes and innovative ways of structuring financial aid payments can be helpful. But Dr. Morest argues that solutions to the financial problems of community college students are "more likely to be programmatic than monetary." She suggests that there is potential in the expansion of internships and service learning. An expansion of coordination with community based organizations can also offer many benefits to students and colleges.

But little progress will be made if reform is limited to the implementation of a series of individual programs and practices. Dr. Morest makes a distinction between the "technology" of reform and the "culture" of reform. The technology of reform involves finding specific successful practices such as learning communities and statewide articulation agreements, but "replicating and broadening the impact of successful technologies involves culture." Culture is crucial. Peter Drucker, quoted in the book, observed, "culture eats strategy for breakfast." Dr. Morest advocates a focus on cultural change in three areas: accountability, curriculum and teaching, and working in networked organizational structures.

The focus on accountability primarily involves more sophisticated and integrated use of data and information. Extensive use of information must become an internalized function of the colleges, but it must also support the alignment and integration of the goals of policy makers, administrators, faculty, and staff.

Community colleges, and higher education in general, are many years behind the K-12 sector in research and analysis of teaching. Much more attention needs to be paid to effective teaching practices, establishing and evaluating learning outcomes, and the creation and measurement of degree pathways and clearly articulated information systems to help students and faculty understand where students are in their programs. A focus on the classroom is crucial for community colleges because that is the most important and sometimes the only significant point of contact between the student and the college.

Reform in community colleges, and indeed in many organizations, is often confined to specific practices that fail to influence the core functioning of the institutions. Often funded by foundations or public sector grants, attracting the activist faculty, these reforms come and go as funding and interest ebbs and flows. Real change requires more thorough organizational transformation, and this may be particularly difficult in community colleges, organizations that must motivate and answer to a variety of constituencies, each with different goals and different levels of influence and power within or over the colleges. Faculty members are fundamental to any significant improvement, but administrators have limited power and influence over them. Yet, despite these challenges, Dr. Morest argues that there is a growing understanding about how organizations change and learn from each other that can be drawn on to help bring about comprehensive improvements in student outcomes in community colleges.

Policy makers, private funders, business leaders, and the public in general have all become more convinced about the important role that community colleges play in providing wider educational opportunity and in preparing an effective workforce and citizenry. Research has played an increasingly important role in identifying the problems and devising and evaluating the solutions. Vanessa Smith Morest has done a masterful job in building on the growing base of research to advance our understanding of these institutions and to develop a broad plan for improving their performance. Her book will be useful to students, researchers, public officials, and college administrators and faculty as they work to serve the interests of millions of community college students nationwide.

Thomas Bailey
Community College Research Center, Teachers College,
Columbia University

Chapter One

Understanding the "Community's" College

Community colleges possess a comparatively short but rich history in the United States. Public two-year colleges first emerged at the beginning of the twentieth century with the establishment of Joliet Junior College in 1901. From that time until the middle of the century the number of institutions grew as the sector gained legitimacy in higher education. By the late 1940s, community colleges arrived at a new milepost. A report published by the President's Commission on Higher Education (the Truman Commission) called for equality of opportunity in American education and gave community colleges the role of ensuring access.[1] Throughout the 1950s to the 1970s, community college enrollment grew rapidly and the principle of the "open door" became a well-established feature of the American postsecondary education system.[2]

Community colleges now play a prominent role as providers of undergraduate education enrolling over seven million students each fall. Overall, they educate more than fifty percent of the undergraduates at public institutions and just over 40 percent of all undergraduates.[3] This is a time of unprecedented interest in higher education and for many students community colleges represent an opportunity to pursue educational goals and aspirations previously beyond reach. Community colleges are low cost, close to home and offer a broad range of courses and curricula in a variety of formats. Students can choose to enroll full-time or part-time, attend during the day or evening, in classes on campus or online, and choose either credit or noncredit status. The admission process is user-friendly and involves filling out a small number of forms, taking necessary placement tests, and paying for classes, all of which can be done up until the last possible moment at many institutions.

As a result, community colleges enroll a highly diverse population of students. Students are considered matriculated even though placement tests reveal academic deficits that indicate their skills are not yet at college level. Community college students may be in their teens or senior citizens, affluent or financially disadvantaged, academically talented or underprepared, but are blended into courses and curricula as they pursue a variety of goals. Some enroll to complete a course or two, others a certificate or Associate degree, and for many, transfer to a four-year institution.

THE PARADOX OF SUCCESS

Unquestionably community colleges represent a major success story in American higher education. As George Vaughan described them in 2005, "What is wrong with the community college today? Not much, seemingly. To the contrary, community colleges are on a roll. Enrollments are booming; prestige is high; public support is unwavering; resources, though far from adequate, continue to flow; courses and programs are, for the most part, current; and much of the rest of higher education finally acknowledges the importance of community colleges in the loosely connected confederation of colleges and universities that constitutes American higher education." But he goes on to say, "somewhere along the way, something went wrong."[4]

While community colleges have a great track record for expansion, their graduation rates lag far behind those of public four-year colleges. Of first-time, full-time, degree-seeking students starting in fall 2005, only 20.6 percent graduated within a three year period (which is 150 percent of time to graduation). Even more problematic, graduation rates are as low as 12 percent for African-American students and 14–16 percent for Hispanic students.[5] This has not gone unnoticed by funding agencies and policy makers. The past decade has seen growing interest in marginal student outcomes and intensified efforts to hold community colleges accountable for both access and completion.

When I started studying community colleges in the late 1990s, student success was not the focal point of dialogue on campus. The focus at that time was on institutional success. For years, social scientists had been trying to draw attention to the low completion and transfer rates of community college students, but their impact was limited because their concerns were largely structural. The perspective that students were not successful at community colleges was framed in large part by a belief that the point of comparison should be four-year colleges and universities.[6] In addition, there were concerns that community colleges were over-extending their resources by continually broadening their mission. Breneman and Nelson, in their 1981 analysis of the financing of community colleges, saw the need to establish priorities as a means for strengthening and improving quality at community colleges.[7] Brint and Karabel and Dougherty argued that, based on research findings, outcomes of students starting at community colleges were inferior to those of students similar in background and characteristics starting at four-year colleges.[8]

Dougherty's analysis defines community college outcomes in terms of economic benefits, freshman and sophomore year attrition, failure to transfer, and attrition after transfer. He found that "community colleges have a contradictory impact on the educational futures of students" because students aspiring to a bachelor's degree attain fewer bachelor's degrees and fewer years of education as compared to those starting at four-year institutions, while students who aspire to less than a bachelor's degree "appear to complete more years of education, but perhaps fewer baccalaureate degrees."[9]

This contradiction poses a formidable challenge to community colleges and the learners they enroll. The majority of today's high school graduates report that they plan to earn a bachelor's degree, but student aspirations are not always well informed. What students think they need to do and what they realistically need to do in order to achieve educational and career goals are often out of alignment.[10] Students enter higher education with multiple options for choice of institution, program, and degree—a characteristic that Brint and Karabel describe as "one of the most distinctive features of an American educational system that is open because it gives students with undistinguished academic records multiple chances to succeed".[11] Burton Clark described the downside of this system as embedded in the role that community colleges must play in delivering disappointment to students: "the conflict between open-door admission and performance of high quality often means a wide discrepancy between the hopes of entering students and the means of their realization…while some students of low promise are successful, for large numbers failure is inevitable and structured."[12]

While academics have fixated on the transfer and vocational roles of community colleges, practitioners and policy makers have placed their emphasis elsewhere. The comprehensive mission of community colleges has made it possible for colleges to emphasize their success in providing access and service to broad segments of the population. It has simultaneously diverted attention from long-term outcomes such as Associate degree completion. The absence, until recently, of a public policy focus on student outcomes can be traced to the growing popularity of community colleges and effective advocacy by college leaders and national associations.

Reliable information about student outcomes at community colleges has been made all the more opaque by the absence of definitions and data regarding student success. Outcomes data can be gleaned from national surveys, as it is today, but these surveys are limited in scope and accessibility. In 1997, when I first started visiting community colleges to conduct research for the

Community College Research Center at Columbia University, I would find myself in the offices of institutional research directors aggregating data in fact books and accreditation self-studies as evidence of the demographic and programmatic characteristics of community colleges. I could readily obtain counts of the number of degrees conferred by major. Occasionally, I could obtain "bits" of information about transfer students based on small-scale inquiries carried out by colleges. Course completion rates, cohort analyses, and breakdowns of both by student background characteristics such as race and age were limited or nonexistent.

At most midsize and small colleges, it was impossible to get numbers beyond the basic descriptive data reported to the Integrated Postsecondary Educational Data System (IPEDS).[13] In many cases, I would find myself talking to the registrar or a college vice president who would explain the complexities of accessing data. This would be accompanied by an awkward commentary on the student information system, reflecting frustration and confusion with a system that seemed to take so much and give so little. At some colleges I would find social scientists delighted with the opportunity to vent their frustration about data with a colleague. Occasionally I found myself confronted by a bureaucrat whose fondest wish would be that I vacate their office as soon as possible. The language of student outcomes did not exist in the colleges that I visited in the late 1990s. Success was defined in terms of enrollment, diversity of programs and services, campus facilities, economic development initiatives, and institutional resources.

Institutional success does not necessarily equate to student success when it comes to community colleges. Part of the popularity of community colleges stems from the comprehensiveness of their mission that allows them to touch so many lives. Community colleges find their way into people's lives one way or another: whether it is through continuing education classes, public events held on campus, English language classes, classes for children, or the year that their friend's son spent there before transferring to university. College presidents serve on a variety of local boards as a way of strengthening connections with the community and garnering local support. Community colleges may not be perceived as high status in comparison to selective colleges and universities, but they are highly valued within their local communities.

Beginning in 2002, the public gained access to more and better information about higher education. Specifically, the Student Right-to-Know (SRK) and Campus Security Act, which was an amendment to the 1965 Higher Education Act, required reporting of graduation statistics. Starting with the cohort entering in 1999, colleges were required to report graduation rates to IPEDS on an annual basis.[14]

Based on local experience, faculty and staff of community colleges must have had some inkling of the information SRK would reveal. After all, if a college enrolls 4,000 first-time students each year but only 400 are awarded degrees at graduation, it is clear that attrition has occurred somewhere along the line, perhaps as a function of part-time course taking patterns, transfer, or employment prior to degree completion. And it was not as if high rates of attrition were unheard of in community colleges. Among campus constituencies and knowledgeable public officials, it was generally understood that graduation was one of the less likely outcomes for community college students. Researchers were also in the know because data from various national surveys indicated low completion rates, low transfer rates, and low levels of college credit earned.

LIFTING THE VEIL OF MYSTERY SURROUNDING GRADUATION RATES

SRK graduation rates for all colleges are collected by the National Center for Education Statistics (NCES) as part of the IPEDS postsecondary data reporting system. A cohort consists of new college students attending college for the first time. Since part-time enrollment would impact the time it takes to graduate, the cohort is further narrowed to first-time, full-time, degree-seeking students. This is the definition used by all colleges and universities nationwide to submit data to IPEDS. However, because of the high rate of part-time attendance at community colleges, the first-time, full-time cohort may be a relatively small proportion of overall enrollment in a college. For example, one out of five students (20 percent) of the 2009 entering student population at Macomb Community College in Michigan was a first-time, full-time, degree-seeking student, while more than four out of five (87 percent) of the entering students at the University of Michigan, Ann Arbor were first-time, full-time, degree-seeking.[15] So, graduation rates that are the basis for assessment of student success at community colleges actually represent outcomes for a small percentage of students overall.

The National Center for Higher Education Management Systems (NCHEMS) provides an excellent online resource for reviewing student data and national graduation rates through its Information Center.[16] NCHEMS data reveal results that vary widely among community colleges throughout the nation. Connecticut currently ranks at the bottom, with a graduation rate of 11.7 percent, while South Dakota graduates 60.7 percent of its community college students. If the focus is shifted to states with the highest community college enrollments, we see that only three (Florida, Arizona, and California) had graduation rates above the national average of 29.2 percent in 2009 (see table 1.1).

Variation among the states suggests that context is important. For example, institutional remediation policies affect graduation rates because the rates are based on a short time frame of three years. Since remedial courses do not count toward a college degree, the number of remedial courses a student is required to take often results in a delay. Many students find themselves taking two or more remedial courses, which can delay enrollment in degree credit courses by a semester or a year or more. African American and Hispanic students place into remedial courses at higher rates than other learners, so states with high proportions of students of color enrolled in community colleges tend to have higher remediation rates and hence lower graduation rates. It is also possible for students to start full-time and switch to part time yet remain in the original SRK cohort. Therefore, states in which the cost of living is high may have more students working full-time during college and hence lower graduation rates. In the state of Connecticut, where the cost of living and competition for jobs is high, two-thirds of community college students attend part-time. Statistics on the proportion of students switching from part-time to full-time are difficult to obtain, but at my college (Norwalk Community College) about 24 percent of students make a change of this type within the course of a semester.

Curriculum can also have a significant impact on graduation rates, which may account for difficultly in assessing differences across institutions. Some occupational programs (for example, those with short-term certificates) may have higher graduation rates, particularly if there are licensing incentives to earn a credential. The economy can have a bearing on graduation rates. In a weak economy where the supply of workers outweighs demand, evidence of having completed a college degree may carry more value on a résumé. Transfer policies also have implications for completion rates. In states and systems with strong articulation agreements that provide direct incentives for degree completion, graduation rates may be higher. Whereas in state systems where articulation is at the course or program level, students may be incentivized to leave the community college once all transferable credits have been earned, even if this means not completing a degree.

FROM STUDENT RIGHT TO KNOW TO EVERYONE WANTS TO KNOW

Analyses of graduation rates conducted at the individual institution level typically go well beyond those available through IPEDS as they are calculated for different purposes. For example, an institution may have its own internal measures, a state may have accountability reporting requirements, accrediting agencies have specific requirements, and grants are generally awarded with accountability measures involving graduation rates for specified learner populations. Upon reviewing data from my own institution, I was able to identify six graduation rates, each based on different cohorts and submitted to different agencies. The results all told a similar story, but varied as much as three percentage points from one another which is significant when a graduation rate is below 20 percent.

Table 1.1 Selected Graduation Rates

SRK Graduation Rate 2006 cohort

Florida	48.1
Arizona	39.3
California	38.2
Ohio	27.1
Texas	25.4
Illinois	25.2
New York	21.4
North Carolina	20.5
Michigan	15.2

Source: NCHEMS Information Center for Higher Education, Policymaking and Analysis at www.higheredinfo.org

State governments, private foundations and federal initiatives have their own definitions of graduation rate because Student Right to Know is limited in terms of its capacity to measure the productivity of community colleges. [17] The composition of a cohort can vary depending on college definitions of first-time students and programs considered to be degree-seeking. For example, when students attend multiple institutions, it is conceivable that they may be represented in more than one cohort. It is logical, therefore, that the SRK definition of graduation rate is an underestimation of actual graduation rates. [18]

Standard reporting systems, in an effort to provide more insight into graduation rates, break information down into multiple categories. For example, graduation rates are routinely reported by race or ethnicity, gender, age, full- and part-time attendance and so on. This can be a tedious process from the standpoint of analyzing, reporting, and interpreting data. Without statistical tests, it is impossible to know whether the results are reliable and are capable of comparison to another cohort. For example, a difference of five percentage points in the graduation rates of Hispanic and non-Hispanic students could be due to the fact that more Hispanic students enrolled full-time in a particular semester. Unfortunately, it is fair to say that at the institutional level the extensive time and effort required to calculate graduation rates is yielding little in the way of new information.

BEYOND GRADUATION RATES

While it is indisputable that graduation rates are significantly lower at community colleges than the general public might expect, the implications for students are less well understood. One of the problems with graduation rate as a measure of student success is that there are multiple outcomes that represent success for community college students. It has long been the contention of community college leaders and staff that student goals must drive any analysis of success, because what could be more meaningful than helping students achieve their goals and aspirations no matter what they might be. This perspective addresses the heterogeneity of student populations and goals, and also assumes that students fully understand the wide range of choices available to them.

Indeed, community college students attend college with a wide range of intentions. Most applications for admission list anywhere from four to twelve "reasons for attending." Cohen and Brawer tackled this issue and concluded that community colleges did not evolve with graduation as a primary goal:

> Studies of student dropout may be only marginally relevant to an institution that regards accessibility as its greatest virtue. The community colleges have organized themselves around the theme of ease in entrance, exit, and reentry. Having made a considerable effort to recruit students and offer them something useful, most faculty members and administrators do want to keep them enrolled, at least until degree or program objectives have been fulfilled. But it is difficult for an institution built on the theme of easy access to limit easy exit. [19]

Once again, we return to the problem of institutional success versus student success. The success of community colleges as institutions was built on access, flexibility, and growth. Under this definition, success for a student would entail having a broad range of options leading many to enroll in community colleges as an avenue for fulfilling their educational needs—a fact that has not gone unnoticed by scores of students enrolling in community colleges who already hold college degrees. The emphasis on access embedded in institutional conceptions of success has opened the door to learners coming for a multitude of reasons, many of which do not culminate in a college degree. Community colleges are convenient entry/exit institutions for learners taking a few courses to upgrade a specific occupational skill or earning general education credits while attending another college or university. The latter is increasingly significant as a way in which students take advantage of the ease of entry and exit described by Cohen and Brawer.

One approach to understanding the importance of Associate degree completion for students is to analyze differences in earnings for students who complete a degree compared to those who do not. This has been described by economists as the "sheepskin effect." The focal question for researchers examining the sheepskin effect is whether there is an added benefit to obtaining an Associate degree above and beyond the earned credit hours. To answer this question, researchers measure the lifetime earnings of students with and without college degrees.[20] The results show earning gains for community college students regardless of degree completion and a small added benefit if the degree is completed.[21] Noteworthy is the finding that credits earned have a positive effect on earning gains.

The complexity of working with a broad range of student outcomes has contributed to a growing number of stakeholders becoming involved in efforts to define and measure student success. These efforts fall under the rubric of accountability and their stated purpose is to inform the public about the performance of community colleges. The following are examples of ongoing efforts to refine and expand the definition of student success at community colleges:

Student Right to Know: Although graduation rate is the focal indicator of student success for SRK, this measure has also been expanded over time. Colleges currently report on retention and transfer rates and the proportion graduating within 200 percent of time to degree (four years at two-year colleges and eight years at four-year colleges and universities). These rates are disaggregated by gender and race. Part-time rates are now also routinely reported.[22]

Voluntary Framework of Accountability (VFA): With Kent Phillipe, Associate Vice President of Research and Student Success at the American Association of Community Colleges (AACC), taking the lead, the VFA seeks to provide measures of graduation, transfer, retention, credit earning, non-credit enrollments, student learning outcomes, and economic contributions. The VFA currently consists of three- and six-year measures.[23]

The Committee on Measures of Student Success: A federally appointed fifteen-member committee of college officials and policy experts led by Tom Bailey (Professor of Economics at Teachers College Columbia University and Director of the Community College Research Center). The Committee first met in October of 2010 and was charged with recommending "additional or alternative measures of student success that are comparable alternatives to the completion or graduation rates of entering degree-seeking, full-time undergraduate students."[24]

Complete College America (CCA): Envisioned and developed by the National Governors' Association as the product of a meeting convened by NCHEMS and the State Higher Education Executive Officers (SHEEO) in summer of 2009. Measures developed by CCA are intended to inform, analyze, show progress, and hold students, institutions and states accountable to the general public and policy makers who invest in higher education.[25]

All of these efforts are based on a fundamental assumption that community college outcomes are more diverse than simply graduation. All include transfer without a degree and retention rates as indicators of success. The VFA and Complete College America initiatives also measure success in remediation, completion of remedial courses, credit accumulation, and course completion. While Student Right to Know uses three- and four-year windows to calculate graduation rates, VFA uses three- and six-year windows and Complete College America uses three- and four-year windows.

THE DEVIL IS IN THE DETAILS

A problem in defining success rates is determining which group of students (or cohort) will comprise the denominator.[26] The denominator not only has implications for the results and their interpretation, but for institutional researchers as well, because data for new student cohorts must be organized according to precise definitions. Student Right to Know, as mentioned earlier, is based on first-time, full-time degree-seeking students. Many first-time students are categorized in college information systems as nondegree seeking because they have not declared a major. At the time of publication, Complete College America did not include nondegree seeking students, but along with VFA included both full- and part-time students. This is handled by disaggregating data so that rates are calculated for both categories of students.

Although colleges invest thousands of person-hours and significant resources in calculating and recalculating success rates for external agencies, definitions of success do appear to be coalescing in terms of quantitative measures used to calculate success rates. There is general agreement that since relatively few students reach graduation, it is necessary to measure their progress at earlier points. Among these "milestones" is success in reaching college level courses for students in remediation. There is also general acknowledgment that enrollment patterns such as part-time attendance and stop-out can be incorporated into success measures, and that neither should be defined as failure.

The success of community college students, however, is much broader than the information captured through student information systems. The ladder of success is characterized by four transitional stages in ascending order. First there is the period of initial enrollment that begins with a process of anticipatory socialization, when students begin to imagine life as a college student and ultimately develop an understanding of the policies and expectations of the particular college they plan to attend. The next rung on the ladder involves the segment of a college career that is captured by data—completion of remediation, course success, and the credit earning which will move a student steadily toward completion. The third rung involves completion. This is the transition that students undertake as they either complete a degree and move into the workforce, or transfer to a four-year college or university. For many students this is a much more fluid process than one would imagine, in which they "swirl" in the educational system—taking courses at more than one institution or continuing to work while they pursue a degree. Finally, there is success in the workforce and the extent to which a community college degree prepares students with the skills that will allow them to pursue a career trajectory.

ORGANIZATION OF THE BOOK

We know more now than ever before about causative factors underlying student failure and attrition. This book is organized around this body of work. Arguably, the difficulties faced by community colleges and their students begin with remedial education. Nationwide, estimates suggest that more than six out of ten new, first-time community college students start in remediation.[27] Some students can expect to log as many as four to six semesters of remedial mathematics, reading, or writing before they are prepared for college-level classes. Indeed, for many students, the remedial classroom comprises the full extent of their college experience, as course completion eludes many students.[28] Chapter 2 reviews the current research on the success rates of students in remediation. Strategies being used by colleges to improve success rates in remediation are examined (for example, self-paced remediation) along with examples drawn from colleges employing these strategies.

Much of the popularity of community colleges rests on the fact that they are local and inexpensive. One unintended consequence of low cost and convenience, however, is the minimal time spent on campus by students. Limited engagement in campus life has implications for success, particularly if success is measured in terms of retention. Chapter 3 focuses on social integration and community college initiatives around retention. In addition to reviewing theory and research on efforts to integrate students into campus life, this chapter examines instruments for measuring student engagement, among them the Community College Survey of Student Engagement (CCSSE) and the Survey of Entering Student Engagement (SENSE).

Chapter 4 turns to the role of career and technical education in community colleges and its effects on student success. In response to low graduation rates, leaders indicate that students come to college to take specific courses or sequences of courses, but not to complete degrees. In fact, students enrolled in career and technical programs often have stronger incentives to graduate, such as certification and a clearly defined curriculum, which are characteristics that researchers believe may increase success rates.[29] Unfortunately, the value of career planning and occupational coursework is often overlooked by administrators and poorly understood by students, despite the fact that community college students come to college to prepare for employment and a career. As community colleges search for motivators that will keep students in college until they graduate or transfer, career and technical education should not be overlooked.

Much of the curriculum at community colleges is aimed at preparing students to complete degrees elsewhere, which has led to confusion and frustration in measuring community college success. Chapter 5 looks at the scope of transfer and the phenomenon of "swirling" from the perspective of student success.[30] This chapter pays special attention to state policies that impact transfer and shape our understanding of student success.[31]

Unless community colleges abandon access, strategies for improving success must involve organizational change. Chapter 6 looks at the topic of student success from the standpoint of theories on organizational change. This chapter provides an overview of internal and external barriers to change, and levers that can help to remove these barriers. Adoption of innovation is a process that moves through a series of predictable stages—a way of thinking about innovation that provides a useful framework for planning and implementing student success initiatives.

FROM BOARDROOMS TO CLASSROOMS

Ultimately, this book is about cultural change leading to educational reform at community colleges. While enrollment growth at community colleges has been impressive, it does not equate with success if the door is revolving and more than half of the students exit before completion. It is clear from the evidence that some of the challenges facing community college students are well beyond the control of institutions. Weak academic preparation and financial difficulties are mountains that community colleges will not be able to move no matter how hard they try.

Chapter 6 addresses the dilemma facing our colleges when they are asked to solve major social problems and respond to ever-increasing numbers of students on shrinking budgets. Think organizational change and inter-institutional cooperation to increase efficiency and productivity).[32] Yet organizational change in public education has historically been a difficult and slow process. In order to enhance the likelihood that students in our colleges will experience success, organizations at every level of the educational system will need to work together in integrated and goal-driven relationships to bring about cultural change.

Experience and social science research tell us that cultural change is unlikely to occur as a result of top-down mandates. Evidence suggests that in many cases reform comes through programs or interventions that reach only small segments of the student population.[33] If the evolution of community colleges over the past century tells us anything, it is that student success runs the risk of being added as yet another mission of our colleges in contrast to a fundamental change in perspective or practice within institutions. In other words, rather than a paradigm shift, the student success movement may represent the latest wave of mission accretion in community colleges.

This trajectory can be changed so that community colleges can perform the role envisioned for them by the public and policy makers through alignment from boardrooms to classrooms. The boardrooms are not only those of individual colleges, but those of the American Association of Community Colleges and the League for Innovation, state and federal departments of education, and private foundations to name a few. The members of these boards have been extraordinarily busy during the past decade traveling around the country spending hours in meetings to investigate, debate, and discuss the future of community colleges. Likewise, those on college campuses have spent countless hours doing the same thing. In order for real change to occur, decisions made at the highest levels must align with those being made on the front lines. After all, it is community college faculty and staff who provide the advice, learning opportunities, and assessments that will shape student outcomes. Much of the power to bring about needed change rests in their hands.

My research and experience in the area of community college student success leads me to believe that three cultural shifts are necessary to scale up and institutionalize the reforms currently underway. First, the dynamics of academic and social integration must be understood and prioritized on community college campuses. In the interest of open access and the belief that students should have a vast array of options available to them, community colleges have lost sight of the fact that the social and psychological processes of becoming a college student are a valuable experiences that shape students' lives. Integration may happen through a wide range of activities including learning communities, student success courses, e-portfolios, social media, community service, and campus activities to name a few. Colleges need to be intentional about helping students forge social bonds and ensuring that students understand there are people on campus, both staff and students, who know and care about them and their academic pursuits.

Second, leadership models need to be developed that foster teamwork. The private sector has moved away from top-down, bureaucratic management, and it is time for the public sector to do the same. Thinking needs to be horizontal rather than vertical when it comes to implementing change; we need to be imagining the work of improving student success in terms of teams rather than committees. Community colleges are complex organizations in which staff play highly specialized roles. An interdisciplinary team might be composed of administrators, staff, faculty, and students and cover both academic and student affairs. Institutional research personnel should be represented on teams even though research offices are spread thin as account-ability and reporting requirements continue to increase. It is increasingly important, however, to develop evaluation expertise college-wide. For this reason, I have included information about data sources and uses throughout each chapter of the book with the hope that this information will make it easier to understand the foundation from which knowledge about student outcomes is taking shape. Analysis and interpretation of data needs to be-come a fundamental skill of college leaders, not simply something left to "back office" staff.

Third, community colleges need to adopt a theory of change that incorpo-rates elements of continuous improvement. The notion that reform can be implemented perfectly from the start is not supported by the literature. Change takes time and unfolds predictably, which can actually strengthen the likelihood of successful implementation. Developing a theory about how reform occurs on campus will make it more likely that scale can be achieved in our efforts. Without a roadmap, it is easy to give up too early or to wait too long for a strategy to take effect that is not working. [34]

Northern Essex Community College (NECC) in Massachusetts provides an example of a college which has embraced these cultural shifts, and there are others as well that will be mentioned throughout the book. In 2007, NECC began to use Appreciative Inquiry (AI) as a process for strategic planning. AI is a bottom-up approach to strategic planning that builds con-sensus by focusing on strength-based positive change. In the first round of planning, more than 150 AI interviews were held with college stakeholders and a culminating strategic planning summit drew over 200 members of the college community to develop the plan. The College has been through this process a second time, resulting in a new plan for 2012. This collaborative planning process has been just one of the ways in which NECC demonstrates its commitment to a culture that is focused on student success and evidence-based decision making.

Community colleges are ripe for cultural change. They hold an estab-lished and respected position in the higher education landscape and their tenets of access and low cost are widely accepted. The challenge that col-leges now face is the tension between access and quality. It makes no sense for community colleges to continue to grow if they cannot ensure that enter-ing students will be well served through the college experience. Shrinking state budgets practically mandate that community colleges create new effi-ciencies in strengthening their services. In the future, change will occur through disruptive innovation and redistribution of resources rather than growth.

Disruptive innovation—the process through which new technologies emerge, catch on, and completely change the way we do things—will be the wave of the future. The IT industry has provided many examples in the past two decades—from personal computers to laptops to tablets—of frame-breaking change. Each of these improvements sacrifices something in exchange for lower cost and smaller size. We have learned that we can live with smaller screens and no keyboard if the computer becomes less cumbersome. Not long ago, researchers identified community colleges as a disruptive innovation and they quickly gained in popularity. The time was right and they permanently changed the landscape of American higher education.[35] Now community colleges are themselves in need of innovation. They are a sector in search of scalable educational strategies that can help students succeed, even if it means fundamentally changing how they organize and deliver services.

NOTES

1. John Dale Russell, "Basic Conclusions and Recommendations of the President's Commission on Higher Education," *Journal of Educational Sociology* 22, no. 8 (1949).
2. George A. Baker, III, ed. *A Handbook on the Community College in America: Its History, Mission, and Management* (Westport, CT: Greenwood Press,1994); Arthur M. Cohen and Florence B. Brawer, *The American Community College, Fifth Edition* (San Francisco, CA: Jossey-Bass, 2009).
3. U.S. Department of Education, National Center for Education Statistics, *Condition of Education,* (Washington, DC: Author, 2011), Indicator 8-2011, Table A-8-2.
4. George B. Vaughan, "(over)Selling the Community College: What Price Access?" *Chronicle of Higher Education* 52, no. 10 (2005), B12.
5. U.S. Department of Education, National Center for Education Statistics, *Digest of Education Statistics*, (Washington, DC: National Center for Education Statistics, 2010), Table 341, http://nces.ed.gov/programs/digest/d10/tables/dt10_341.asp.
6. D. E. Leigh and A. M. Gill, "Do Community Colleges Really Divert Students from Earning Bachelor's Degrees?," *Economics of Education Review* 22(2003); Celia E. Rouse, "Democratization or Diversion? The Effect of Junior Colleges on Educational Attainment," *Journal of Business and Economic Statistics* 13(1995).
7. David W. Breneman and Susan C. Nelson, *Financing Community Colleges: An Economic Perspective* (Washington, D.C.: Brookings Institution Press, 1981).
8. Steven Brint and Jerome Karabel, *The Diverted Dream: Community Colleges and the Promise of Educational Opportunity in America, 1900 - 1985* (New York: Oxford University Press, 1989); Kevin J. Dougherty, *The Contradictory College: The Conflicting Origins, Impacts, and Futures of the Community Colleges* (Albany, NY: State University of New York Press, 1994).
9. Dougherty, *The Contradictory College: The Conflicting Origins, Impacts, and Futures of the Community Colleges*, 57.
10. Barbara Schneider and David Stevensen, *The Ambitious Generation: America's Teenagers, Motivated but Directionless* (New Haven, CT: Yale University Press, 2000).
11. Brint and Karabel, *The Diverted Dream: Community Colleges and the Promise of Educational Opportunity in America, 1900 – 1985*, 221.
12. Burton R. Clark, "The 'Cooling-out' Function in Higher Education," *The American Journal of Sociology* 65, no. 6 (1960), 571.

13. U.S. Department of Education, "Integrated Postsecondary Education Data System (IPEDS)," ed. National Center for Education Statistics (Washington, DC).

14. Thomas Bailey, Peter M. Crosta, and Davis Jenkins, "What Can Student Right-to-Know Graduation Rates Tell Us About Community College Performance?" (New York, NY: Community College Research Center, Teachers College, Columbia University, 2006).

15. http://nces.ed.gov/collegenavigator/.

16. http://www.higheredinfo.org/.

17. Thomas R. Bailey, Peter Crosta, and Davis Jenkins, "What Can Student Right-to-Know Graduation Rates Tell Us About Community College Performance?" (New York, NY: Community College Research Center), CCRC Working Paper No. 6.

18. Bailey, Crosta and Jenkins, "What Can Student Right-to-Know Graduation Rates Tell Us About Community College Performance? 4.

19. Arthur M. Cohen and Florence B. Brawer, *The American Community College, Fourth Edition* (San Francisco, CA: Jossey-Bass, 2003), 66.

20. Clive Belfield and Thomas Bailey, "The Benefits of Attending Community College: A Review of the Evidence," *Community college Review* 39, no. 1 (2011); W. Norton Grubb, "The Returns to Education in the Sub-Baccalaureate Labor Market, 1984-1990," *Economics of Education Review* 16 (1997).

21. Belfield and Bailey, "The Benefits of Attending Community College: A Review of the Evidence."; Thomas J. Kane and Celia E. Rouse, "The Community College: Educating Students at the Margin between College and Work," *The Journal of Economic Perspectives* 13, no. 1 (1999).

22. http://nces.ed.gov/collegenavigator/

23. http://www.aacc.nche.edu/Resources/aaccprograms/VFAWeb/default.aspx

24. Committee on Measures of Student Success: A Report to Secretary of Education Arne Duncan, (December, 2011) may be retrieved at www2.ed.gov/about/bdscomm/list/cmss-committee-report-final.pdf.

25. http://www.completecollege.org/

26. Willard C. Hom, "The Denominator as the "Target", *Community College Review* 37, no. 2 (2009).

27. Paul Attewell, Scott Heil, and Liza Reisel, "Competing Explanations of Undergraduate Noncompletion," *American Educationl Research Journal* 48, no. 3 (2011); Thomas Bailey, Dong Wook Jeong, and Sung-Woo Cho, "Referral, Enrollment, and Completion in Developmental Education Sequences in Community Colleges," (New York, NY: Community College Research Center, Teachers College, Columbia University, 2009).

28. Thomas Bailey, "Challenge and Opportunity: Rethinking the Role and Function of Developmental Education in Community College," *New Directors for Community Colleges*, no. 145 (2009).

29. Ann Person and James E. Rosenbaum, "Student Planning and Information Problems in Different College Structures," *Teachers College Record* 108, no. 3 (2006).

30. Clifford Adelman, "The Toolbox Revisited: Paths to Degree Completion from High School through College," (Washington, DC: U.S. Department of Education, 2006).

31. Greg Anderson, Mariana Alfonso, and J. C. Sun, "Rethinking Cooling out at Public Community Colleges: An Examination of Fiscal and Demographic Trends in Higher Education and the Rise of Statewide Articulation Agreements." *Teachers College Record* 108, no. 3 (2006).

32. C. M. Mullin, "Doing More with Less: The Inequitable Funding of Community Colleges," (Washington D.C.: American Association of Communithy Colleges, September 2010).

33. Elizabeth Zachry Rutschow et al., "Turning the Tide: Five Years of Achieving the Dream in Community Colleges," (New York, NY: MDRC, 2011).

34. Barbara Schneider and Sarah-Kathryn McDonald, Eds. *Scale-Up in Education: Issues in Practice*, Volume 11, (New York: Rowman & Littlefield, Inc., 2007).

35. Clayton M. Christensen et al., "Disruptive Innovation for Social Change," *Harvard Business Review*, December (2006).

Chapter Two

Transitioning to College

The fall registration process starts out slowly at Costal Community College. Applications are available year round and students can sign up for September classes starting in April. But by the end of July, classes are only about 45 percent full. Of the new first-time in college (FTIC) students who will begin classes in the fall, only 20 percent have actually registered. The month of August will bring a deluge of thousands of students, many of them enrolling in college for the first time. Costal can expect 80 percent of the new students and 30 to 40 percent of the continuing students to arrive on campus requiring some combination of placement testing, advising, and financial aid within one month of classes starting.

The process of transitioning into college has a unique character at community colleges that has long lasting social and academic consequences for students. As a point of comparison, consider the early transitional experiences of students matriculating in selective four-year colleges. The application process consists of a series of activities including college tours, interviews, essay writing, and comparison shopping. For some students, the process begins to unfold midway through high school. Less selective four-year colleges also encourage these steps of students, although they may be taken in a more circumscribed time frame.

Community colleges, on the other hand, will accept students up to, and even after, the first day of class. The vast majority of community colleges have no admissions requirements other than a high school diploma. As open door institutions, students can simply provide their contact information and cover a small application fee to initiate college attendance. Intake processes are designed to serve a broad range of student needs. According to the National Center for Educational Statistics, approximately 19 percent of the nation's high school graduates transition directly into community colleges—a

change of only 2 percent since 1992.[1] But, these students are only one con-
stituent group. Others include adult learners, many without previous college
experience, students transferring from other institutions, students with specific educational needs such as English as a Second Language or skills upgrad-
ing, senior citizens, and students who are concurrently enrolled in high
school. The goals and expectations of students entering community colleges
are as diverse as the students themselves, but the application process is
streamlined—one size fits all.

Since community colleges do not employ a filter for entering students,
they require a mechanism for determining the academic proficiency of newly
admitted students. A number of different methodologies are used for assessment, depending on state context and institutional policy. The most popular
method is through placement testing with most colleges relying on one of
two well-known testing companies, Accuplacer and COMPASS, to administer placement tests online through testing centers located on college campuses. Testing takes a variety of shapes and forms, but the end result is the
same: students' writing and math levels are assessed and they are placed into
courses according to institutional standards.

In comparison to the application process at four-year colleges and universities, the transition into community college boils down to bare essentials
with the potential to be abrupt and impersonal. Although systems are designed to minimize barriers that might interfere with an individual's ability to
enroll in college, the trade-off is that students have less time for examination
and consideration of program offerings, cross-institutional comparisons, or
reflection on a decision to attend a particular college. Studies dealing with
the topic of why students choose community colleges generally conclude that
the primary reasons are geography and cost. The *Catch-22* for community
colleges is that in order to ensure accessibility, they must surrender the
ability to engage students in a process of anticipatory socialization.

Anticipatory socialization occurs when individuals become accustomed
to the norms, beliefs, and values of a new institutional setting. It is a period
of identity development during which students begin to see themselves as
members of a new group—in this case, students who attend a particular
institution.[2] For most community college students, intake processes do not
address anticipatory socialization and only prepare them to enter an institutional culture characterized by bureaucracy and ambiguity. Admissions and
registration processes come replete with lines, testing, forms and policies,
and classes for which they do not receive college credit. In the process of
settling into classes, students encounter caring faculty and staff who encourage and support their goals and aspirations, but whose efforts are compro-
mised by a matriculation process designed to manage a tidal wave of under-
prepared students—one that has little to do with student success.

Placement into developmental education courses further complicates the process of welcoming new students, as many must be told they are not ready to begin a college curriculum. Since the majority of new students enroll in one or more remedial courses, it is important to understand the breadth and intensity of challenges associated with remediation as a critical first step toward increasing the success rate of community college students.

REMEDIATION: SCOPE AND EXTENT

Several national data sources provide information about the scope of community college remediation. First are large-scale national surveys conducted by the Department of Education, National Center for Education Statistics (NCES). Data are also available in longitudinal student unit data[3] describing remediation in the National Postsecondary Aid Study (NPSAS: 04)[4] and the National Education Longitudinal Survey (NELS: 88).[5] A second source of information is available from NCES through the Postsecondary Education Quick Information System survey (PEQUIS)[6] which provides data on remedial programs. And a third source of information is the Achieving the Dream (ATD database), which has been collecting student unit data on remedial course-taking and outcomes from participating colleges since 2004.

Each of these sources is limited by serious drawbacks. National surveys are effective at allowing researchers and practitioners to predict long-term outcomes, because they have followed large numbers of students over a period of years. They also target scientifically selected samples of students that can be weighted to adjust for underrepresented demographic groups. The shortcoming of national surveys, however, is that students in the database entered college in 1992 for NELS and in 1988 and in 2003 for NPSAS, making both surveys dated by comparison to institutional data. The PEQIS study is also more than a decade old. Achieving the Dream data, while relatively recent, are not drawn from a randomized sample of colleges. Achieving the Dream colleges are selected for participation in the program on the basis of enrollment of disproportionate numbers of low income and minority students, so we cannot assume this sample is generalizable.

Estimates of the scope of remediation at community colleges vary. In their analysis of the NPSAS:2004, Horn and Neville found that 43 percent of first- and second-year students enrolled in public two-year colleges took at least one remedial course.[7] Attewell et al. similarly found that 40 percent of college students in NELS:1988 took at least one remedial course when they arrived at college, which for most was in 1992.[8] In 2000, the PEQIS survey found that 42 percent of entering community college freshmen enrolled in at least one remedial course.[9] This survey, along with the results of Attewell et al., found that mathematics remediation enrolled the largest proportion of

students, followed by writing and reading. The authors also found that remedial placement varies by socioeconomic status. For example, 38 percent of
students from suburban high schools required remediation compared with 52
percent of students from urban high schools. Fifty-two percent of students in
the lowest socioeconomic quarter took remedial coursework compared with
only 24 percent of those in the highest quarter.[10] Results coming out of
Achieving the Dream colleges, which are by definition low income and
minority serving institutions, indicated higher rates of remedial participation.
In the ATD database, 59 percent of students enrolled in at least one developmental course.[11]

STRUCTURAL PROBLEMS WITH CURRICULA

Looking at the structure of remediation within institutions helps to explain
why it is difficult to obtain national averages for remedial participation. In
most states, coordination of community colleges is decentralized, thereby
giving institutions considerable autonomy in the policies surrounding remedial education. Colleges within the same state, sometimes separated by only
a short distance, vary in the cutoff scores they use for placement and the
number of remedial levels offered. Working backward, this would suggest
that there are differences in curricular standards for remediation across colleges. Not only do standards specific to course placement levels differ, but
course sequences do as well.

To illustrate, table 2.1 shows the developmental math sequences of four
community colleges located in the same state. All are within driving distance
of one other, yet there are clear differences in the course sequences, particularly where intermediate algebra is concerned. Prefixes like "pre-algebra,"
"introductory," "intermediate," and "college" indicate different levels, but
making sense of the numbering systems and organization of the curriculum is
challenging even for an expert. Although the terminology in English remediation is more consistent, in that English 101 is typically considered college-
level English, there is still ambiguity about the balance of reading and writing, and standards for college-level English.

From the standpoint of research on community colleges, complicated
course numbering and sequencing makes comparisons among colleges difficult. Add to this the fact that curricula change over time and that students
need to receive a grade of C- or better in remedial courses to move on to the
next level in the sequence, and the task of measurement becomes even more
complicated. Nevertheless, a rich source of data on remediation can be found
in state level data sets, because data are drawn directly from student records.

Students routinely indicate confusion with remedial policies and processes. Deil-Amen and Rosenbaum conducted case studies of two community

Table 2.1 Comparison of Remedial Sequences of Four Community Colleges in the Same State, 2010-2011

Major Urban CC	Rural CC	Small City CC	Suburban CC
084 Basic Math I	089 Fundamentals of Mathematics	021 Pre-Algebra	091 Math Fundamentals
085 Basic Math II	091 Elementary Algebra	022 Basic Algebra	101 Introductory Algebra I
108 Introduction to Algebra	096 Intermediate Algebra	023 Intermediate Algebra	102 Introductory Algebra II
101 Elementary Algebra	108 Modern College Mathematics or	151 College Mathematics or	103 Introductory Algebra III
102 Intermediate Algebra	110 Intro to College Algebra/Trig	175 College Algebra	121 College Algebra
(shaded areas are considered to be college level)			

colleges involving interviews with students (n=130) and faculty and staff (n=54), classroom observations, and archival data to examine how community colleges communicate information about remedial placement to students.[12] They found large gaps in student understanding of under-preparedness for college. Part of this gap could be explained by ambiguous and misleading language and messages typically used by colleges to convey information about placement policies. In an effort to avoid discouraging students, counselors and instructors "neutralize" information (for example, the euphemistic use of "developmental" instead of remedial). Deil-Amen and Rosenbaum also found that students were unclear about the implications of their placement in remedial courses: "Students often go for several months, a full semester, or even a full year without knowing that their remedial courses are not counting toward a degree or transfer goals,"[13] Overall, 73 percent of the students interviewed who had taken remedial courses were unclear or made erroneous assumptions about their remedial status.[14]

Remedial placement policies at community colleges are driven by contextual realities. Federal financial aid programs require students to demonstrate the "ability to benefit" from college education if they cannot provide evidence of a high school diploma. This requirement has been partially responsible for the homogeneity in testing and placement practices and the near-monopoly of two testing companies. Placement policies are further influenced by the large volume of students generated by open admissions. Testing and placement is an efficient process for placing students, compared to collecting and evaluating high school transcripts, as would be standard practice in four-year colleges. Students can be mass-tested electronically in testing centers, which automates placement since the majority of students do not score near the cutoff point. This practice also provides an "objective" way of placing students—an important consideration for colleges that are reliant upon good will and political support in their local communities. Through placement testing, community colleges can avoid the politics of poor academic performance and minimize the negative consequences of fallout for learners and public school districts.

Placement in remediation has important and lasting consequences for community college students. Remediation uses up credits and financial aid. It is also frustrating and demoralizing for students when they discover that remedial courses do not count for college credit or find that they are in a classroom that does not fit their needs. Since community college students typically have background characteristics that put them at risk of failure, each semester of enrollment must be used wisely. The research provides mixed evidence on the efficacy of remediation, as students and institutions walk a tightrope, balancing standards and attrition.

OUTCOMES OF REMEDIATION

There are several ways to think about the outcomes of remediation. One can inquire into the success rates of remedial courses by asking and answering pressing questions: How many students complete the remedial sequence and proceed to college-level courses? How do remedial students perform in college-level courses? What long-term outcomes do students achieve—credits completed, degree and certificate completion, and graduation? These questions are at the heart of a burgeoning research agenda on remediation.

Using Achieving the Dream data, Bailey, Jeong and Cho found that 46 percent of students in ATD colleges enrolled in reading remediation courses and 33 percent in mathematics remediation courses completed developmental education sequences.[15] Completion rates were lower for students placing at lower levels of remediation. They also found that among students completing remedial sequences, 50–55 percent also completed a college level course. However, a significant number of students never enrolled in the college level course. Overall, only 20 percent of the students enrolled in math remediation and 37 percent of those enrolled in reading remediation completed a college level course in those subject areas.[16] Interestingly, Bailey, Jeong and Cho found that a small proportion of students refused remedial course placement in favor of college level courses, and achieved a pass rate of 72 percent.[17]

Attewell et al. found that 28 percent of remedial students at two-year colleges graduated within 8.5 years compared with 43 percent of non-remedial students.[18] By using a technique called propensity scoring, the researchers were able to parcel out the effects of poor academic preparation in high school from taking remedial courses in college. Propensity scoring is a system in which similar students who did and did not receive the intervention are statistically matched. This allows researchers to eliminate some of the self-selection bias that results from student behavior. Attewell et al. found that the gap in graduation rates between remedial and noremedial students had little to do with taking remedial courses in college. Rather, it was a function of pre-existing skill differences carried over from high school. Furthermore, remedial courses in community colleges were not associated with lower chances of academic success.

Using data from Ohio community colleges, Bettinger and Long were able to compare the outcomes of students who did and did not receive remediation, taking into account differences in placement policies among colleges.[19] While aggregate state data seemed to indicate that students performed poorly if they were placed in remediation, a deep dive analysis revealed that students requiring remediation were weaker students in general. Using a two-step process in which they initially predicted college choice based on geography and then compared students with similar backgrounds and academic preparedness at colleges with different cutoff policies, Bettinger and Long were able to control for some of the bias that would result in nonrandom placement in remediation. The results of this process were mixed. Students participating in math remediation completed more credits, but exhibited an absence of long-term effects on outcomes such as stop-out or degree completion.[20] Results in English remediation were inconclusive, perhaps because it was more difficult for researchers to control for differences in placement policies.

A methodology that has been particularly helpful for analyzing the outcomes of remediation is regression discontinuity. Regression discontinuity assumes that, in the absence of intervention, students who are slightly above and below the cut-off points are otherwise similar with the only difference between them the intervention of remediation. Results are providing interesting insights into the impact of remediation.

In a study of Florida's community colleges, researchers found students requiring mathematics remediation were slightly more likely to persist to the second year than their nonremedial peers.[21] On the other hand, remedial students in English passed college-level English at slightly lower levels than peers who placed directly into college-level English. Overall, the researchers concluded that remediation "might promote early persistence in college, but does not necessarily help community college students on the margin of passing the cutoff make long-term progress toward the degree."[22]

Nationally, roughly one-third of student attempts at remedial coursework end in failure.[23] While quantitative analyses of the outcomes of remediation provide evidence of high dropout rates and poor performance in remedial classes, the reasons for these outcomes are not conclusively known. It is reasonable to surmise, however, that students fare poorly because they are arriving at college with marginal academic capabilities and poorly developed study skills. Also the difficulties and demands that come from being a first-generation or low income college student can take a significant toll. Further complicating these findings is research on long-term outcomes of students referred to but not enrolling in remedial courses suggesting that in some cases remediation may do more harm than good. Most colleges use prerequisite courses as a mechanism for requiring students to take remedial courses. Perin and Charron conducted case studies of the placement practices of fifteen community colleges and found wide variation in formal and informal mechanisms for determining placement levels and progress through remediation.[24] Irrespective of the placement mechanism used, a number of students slip through the system without taking remedial courses and experience mixed levels of success.

WHO OWNS THE PROBLEM?

It is often said that the first step toward self-improvement is acknowledging a problem. Unquestionably, the challenges associated with remediation in community colleges have been acknowledged. Reform efforts have centered on how to improve the remedial outcomes of students and significant resources have been directed toward trying to produce better results for remedial students. However, a question about ownership of "the problem" lingers. Is the high failure rate a problem generated and left unresolved by poor preparation in high schools? Are students themselves to blame? Or, are community colleges failing students through marginal curricula and sub-standard instruction?

What is not at question is the serious condition of remediation in community colleges. The need for remediation in reading, writing, and mathematics is pervasive with as many as two-thirds of the students in entering cohorts requiring remediation. Community colleges can either help or hinder the progress of remedial students depending on how they choose to approach remediation. Evidence of outcomes in this area is extraordinarily mixed. On one hand, students who successfully complete remedial courses appear to do as well as those entering college and taking college-level courses. On the other hand, this is only a small percentage of the students who attempt remediation because most never reach college-level courses. Causative factors underlying this problem are being examined by researchers, policy makers and college personnel alike through research directed toward key problem areas in remediation: (1) Are testing processes flawed thereby resulting in student failure due to inaccurate placement? (2) Are academic performance expectations between high schools and community colleges misaligned? (3) Do developmental curricula that are not contextualized impede student progress?

Students Fail Because:

The Testing Process is Flawed. In the 2003 PEQUIS survey, approximately 92 percent of two-year colleges reported using testing to determine course placement of students. Market research indicates that two major tests dominate the market: the Accuplacer developed by College Board (used by 62 percent of community colleges) and the COMPASS, developed by ACT (used by 46 percent of community colleges).[25] Colleges do not necessarily use one test or the other exclusively, and these tests are often supplemented by local instruments such as "homegrown" tests developed and evaluated by instructors on campus.

When the determination of college readiness relies on measures established by major testing companies, questions invariably arise about instrument validity. What exactly is the test measuring? In their analysis of assessment at community colleges, Hughes and Scott-Clayton identified several limitations of the validity of test measures.[26] One concerns the fact that the determination of validity is based on college course grades, which could result in important outcomes being overlooked such as knowledge acquisition, persistence, and success. Hughes and Scott-Clayton also point out that

> simply confirming that a placement exam predicts performance in college-level math does not, on its own, imply that students with low scores should be assigned to remedial math. This component, often overlooked in practice, is central to the 'actionable assessment' hypothesis—the idea that assessment should identify not just who is struggling, but also who is likely to benefit from a given treatment.[27]

Instructors routinely report high levels of confidence in college placement processes, yet cutoff scores are rarely, if ever, validated. In a recent analysis of the validity of the COMPASS test for placement Scott-Calyton concluded that "using high school achievement alone as a placement screen results in fewer placement mistakes than using test scores alone—substantially so in English—without changing the percentage of students assigned to remediation."[28] A second study, conducted by Belfield and Crosta, produced similar findings.[29]

High Schools and Community Colleges Do Not Work Together. All too many high school students collect diplomas in the spring, only to find out in the fall that they did not place into college-level courses. The 2009 National Curriculum Survey conducted by ACT surveyed 7,680 high school and college teachers about curricula in the areas of English/writing, mathematics, reading, and science.[30] The results showed high levels of disagreement between high school and college instructors on the academic preparedness of students. While 91 percent of high school teachers reported that students were well prepared for college-level work in their content area, only 26 percent of college instructors agreed.[31] When this information was disaggregated by subject area, the results showed the greatest difference of opinion is in English/writing and the least in science. The data revealed a difference in breadth and depth between high school and college with high school teachers

concerned about breadth across subject fields, while college instructors fa-
vored focus and depth in curricula. At a more fundamental level, high school
and college instructors placed different emphases in curricula by assigning
different weights to specific competencies, such as sentence structure in writing and basic operations in mathematics. One of the most informative findings in this study was the indication by high school teachers (42 percent of
those surveyed) that expectations are reduced "a great deal" or "completely"
for students who are not college bound.[32]

Remedial Curricula are Decontextualized. Students are recommended for
placement in remedial courses in order to prepare for the demands of college-
level courses. Many have specific academic goals in mind when they enter
college and when required to learn basic mathematics, reading, and writing,
believe that their time is being wasted.[33] Contextualization—integrating basic skills education in mathematics, reading, or writing into general education
subject matter or occupational courses—can ease this tension by mainstream-
ing students into college-level work. It is also possible to contextualize by
creating assignments in remedial courses that employ the subject matter of a
particular occupation. In this way, students are explicitly preparing for college-level courses they will be taking in future semesters. The results of
efforts to contextualize remediation are generally encouraging as students
who are exposed to contextualized learning are passing classes at higher rates
and earning more credits than those who are not. This is an area, however,
that warrants more study through research that is capable of assessing direct
impact.[34]

IMPROVING SUCCESS IN TRANSITIONING TO COLLEGE

By embracing open access, community colleges have simultaneously opened
themselves to opportunities and challenges implicit in serving a diverse student population. The academic capabilities of students entering community
colleges are incredibly broad, ranging from those with less than an eighth
grade level in mathematics, writing, and reading skills to individuals with
post-graduate degrees. One approach to resolution would be to become more
selective and move remedial education to another sector of the educational
system. This, however, would create yet another educational transition for
students, which would ultimately become another barrier. At the same time,
if community colleges are to continue to provide remediation on a large
scale, careful consideration should be given to what can be done to increase
success rates.

A decade ago, the Lumina Foundation became involved with the problem
of student success in community college remediation. Other foundations followed, working in partnership with the Lumina, including the Bill & Melinda

Gates Foundation, which together with Lumina established the Developmental Education Initiative. Using foundation funds, hundreds of community colleges nationwide have designed and tested strategies for improving remedial outcomes that are starting to yield important results. Some of the more prominent strategies are described below.

Working With High School Students

We know that factors predisposing students to placement in remedial courses are present before college. One logical place to initiate efforts to mitigate the need for remediation, therefore, is through collaboration with high schools. Dual enrollment is currently an option at many high schools nationwide. Some states, such as Florida and Washington, have embraced dual enrollment through state level policies supporting these programs. Dual enrollment enables students to enroll in college before high school graduation through programs that are delivered in a range of formats. Some high schools apply college credits toward high school diplomas whereas others do not. Some high schools offer college courses on their own campuses, some of which are taught by their own teachers (if they meet qualifications to teach at the community college level), while others require students to take courses on the college campus.

A form of dual enrollment with direct implications for remediation is the provision for high school students to take remedial courses while enrolled in high school. Another design calls for high school graduates to take remedial courses during the summer between high school graduation and college entry. These programs are labeled bridge programs because they help students transition to college by minimizing or eliminating the need for remediation once the academic year begins. Another intervention with high school students involves early testing. Early testing programs make it possible for high school students to take placement tests early enough in high school to provide time for corrective action before college entry.

Changing the Structure and Sequence of Remedial Courses

Evidence is mounting that alternative structures may help students successfully navigate and complete remediation.[35] Structural reforms acknowledge that some students may not need a traditional semester of fifteen weeks to master the material in a developmental course. By requiring students to proceed through developmental courses in a traditional format, progress may be retarded to the point of increasing the chances that they will leave college. Students who withdraw from a remedial course must wait several months until the next semester to begin the course again. The result is often a serious loss of momentum as well as foregone potential for learning, because a

student may forget what he or she has been exposed to, particularly if expo-
sure ends prematurely.

One option is to compress remedial courses so that they can be taken in a
shorter time frame. For example, the FastStart program at the University of
Denver combines courses to enable a student to simultaneously move
through multiple courses in a semester. Another method is to modularize the
curriculum so students can demonstrate mastery of remedial skills and move
on to the next module—a strategy employed by Housatonic Community
College in Connecticut and currently being adopted statewide in Virginia.

One of the more innovative methods for speeding students through remediation is the Accelerated Learning Program (ALP) at the Community College of Baltimore County. In this model, developmental students take English 101 with college-ready students and also take an ALP companion course.
The two courses together are six credits, and three credits will count toward a
college degree. The idea is to reduce the amount of time required to complete
English 101 and thus limit the chances of students dropping out prior to
completing the remedial and college-level course. Evaluation of this model is
showing positive results, with students completing English 101 and 102 at
higher rates and exhibiting long-term effects in the form of credits earned in
the subsequent academic year.[36]

Contextualizing Learning

Remedial curricula have become a primary focus of reform efforts in community colleges. In most community colleges, mathematics, reading. and
writing courses are de-contextualized and focused on basic mathematics,
literacy, and writing skills. Students respond with frustration, because course
material does not seem to be moving them toward educational and career
goals. In response, colleges have moved to integrate substantive material into
remedial courses as a way of engaging students and also giving them an
opportunity to begin a college-level curriculum. Increasingly common are
efforts to contextualize curricula by pairing remedial courses with college-
level courses at the program level.

The Washington State Integrated Basic Education and Skills Training (I-
BEST) program provides an example of course pairing. Through the I-BEST
program, students are exposed to a curriculum that contextualizes remediation within a workforce training curriculum. Courses are taught by teams of
basic skills and technical/professional instructors. State-level data indicate
that I-BEST students earned more college credit after three years than a
comparison group of students (Zeidenberg, Cho, & Jenkins, 2010; Wachen,
Jenkins, & Van Noy, 2010).[37]

The Carnegie Foundation for the Advancement of Teaching's Statway™
project is another large scale effort toward contextualization. Statway™ is a

year-long pathway moving students through developmental mathematics and into college level mathematics through statistics, data analysis, and quantitative reasoning. The premise of the program is that statistical skills and perspectives are essential for most occupational and professional fields. The Statway™ curriculum emphasizes applied knowledge as a way of promoting public discussion about learning and math anxiety. The key to this program is real data sets that students use throughout the curriculum, because "working with real data rewards students with answers to interesting research questions, thereby increasing their motivation to complete the task. Real data brings students as close as possible to the actual research experience, and provides an opportunity to teach them how to solve problems that arise in practice."[38] Although it is too early to determine the effectiveness of Statway™ in producing learning gains, initial indications are positive.

Strengthening Research and Assessment

There is little doubt that the national focus on remediation is producing insights through research with important implications for practice. However, it is critical that institutions conduct their own research on remediation to discern progress at the institutional level. As described earlier, remediation is highly contextualized. While national studies can draw on self-report and transcript data to obtain a profile on remediation, at the campus level there is the opportunity to interact with students and instructors directly and get an unobstructed view of the impact of interventions.

A useful tool for campus-level inquiry emerging out of national research on remediation is the use of "momentum points" as a means for assessing performance and progress. This methodology is based on a conceptualization by Ewell,[39] which identifies *milestones*, or "measurable educational achievements that include both *conventional terminal completions*, such as earning a credential or transferring to a baccalaureate program, and *intermediate outcomes*, such as completing developmental education or adult basic skill requirements."[40] Researchers identify a cohort of students—typically new, first-time students starting in the fall semester—and measure the rate at which students reach momentum points based on milestones. Examples of momentum points include: the percentage of remedial students successfully completing their remedial sequence during the first two years of college; the percentage that successfully complete a college-level course within three years; and, the percentage earning thirty credits within three years. Cohorts can be broken down into specific student subgroups (for example, degree students only) and disaggregated in order to observe differences among students according to age, race, and gender.

Student learning outcomes assessment (SLO) will play an increasingly important role in remediation. Remedial courses should create a pathway for students to follow from pre-college to college-level work. A starting point for improving remediation, therefore, would be clearly articulated and measurable learning outcomes for each course level in remediation. Results should be made available to students and to K–12 schools, because communication with high school districts can be improved through the articulation of standards. Careful assessment of student progress against student learning outcomes will enable institutions to diagnose reasons why students are performing poorly. This would provide instructors with an opportunity to discuss curricula and areas in which students require intensive remediation, so that they are prepared to succeed at the next level.

IMPLICATIONS FOR STUDENT SUCCESS

While as a nation we are starting to make headway into understanding community college remediation, there is still much work to be done. In particular, improved qualitative research methodologies are needed to elicit information on why students are failing or withdrawing from remedial courses. Advanced evaluation work is also needed. The techniques of propensity scoring and regression discontinuity are providing critical methodological rigor, but there is still much to be done in evaluating the effect of interventions employed in colleges across the country. Although complex statistical techniques are impractical for many researchers, it is critically important that colleges find new and better ways to evaluate remedial efforts.[41]

What we are likely to learn through research is that students bring severe skill deficits to college. Further, traditional approaches to remediation will not be adequate for resolving some of these deficits. Although we conceive of developmental skills coursework as "remediation," which implies a quick brush-up or a solvable problem, it is likely that many students are attending an open-door college because they have chronic mathematics, writing, or reading difficulties. For some, this is the result of learning disabilities, for others it may be weak preparation. Either way, fifteen weeks of classroom time is unlikely to move a student from an eighth grade to tenth grade level if he or she experienced difficulty while enrolled in high school.

We are also likely to learn that remediation is a large-scale problem that requires large-scale solutions. If the majority of students entering a college with 10,000 students require remediation, the college will have close to 2,000 new remedial students each fall semester, of whom 1,200 are likely to fail and drop out unless there is systemic change. Given these numbers, it is unlikely that there will be a "silver bullet" because a significant part of the problem is the diversity of student needs and capabilities. Community colleges must be prepared to initiate and manage a wide variety of interventions carried out by instructors and staff who possess an energy and tenacity suitable to the task.

NOTES

1. NCES, "Condition of Education: Closer Look," (Washington, DC: National Center for Education Statistics, 2008).

2. Melinda Mechur Karp, *Facing the Future: Identity Development among College Now Students* (New York, NY: Dissertation, Columbia University, 2006).

3. Longitudinal refers to a survey design that follows the same student over time. Student unit data refers to a dataset in which the individual student is the unit of analysis. Each student has a unique identification number, which makes it possible for a researcher to keep track of what that student does longitudinally.

4. See http://nces.ed.gov/surveys/npsas/.

5. See http://nces.ed.gov/surveys/nels88/.

6. See http://nces.ed.gov/surveys/peqis.

7. L. Horn and S Nevill, "Profile of Undergraduates in U.S. Postsecondary Education Institutions: 2003-04: With a Special Analysis of Community College Students," (Washington, DC: National Center for Education Statistics, 2006).

8. Paul Attewell, Scott Heil, and Liza Reisel, "Competing Explanations of Undergraduate Noncompletion," *American Educationl Research Journal* 48, no. 3 (2011).

9. Basmat Parsad and Laurie Lewis, "Remedial Education at Degree-Granting Postsecondary Institutions in Fall 2000," (Washington, DC: U.S. Department of Education, National Center for Education Statistics, 2003).

10. Attewell, Heil, and Reisel, "Competing Explanations of Undergraduate Noncompletion," 899.

11. Thomas Bailey, Dong Wook Jeong, and Sung-Woo Cho, "Referral, Enrollment, and Completion in Developmental Education Sequences in Community Colleges," (New York, NY: Community College Research Center, Teachers College, Columbia University, 2009).

12. Regina Diel-Amen and James E. Rosenbaum, "The Unitended Consequences of Stigma-Free Remediation," *Sociology of Education* 75, July (2002).

13. Ibid., 260.

14. Ibid., 262.

15. Bailey, Jeong, and Cho, "Referral, Enrollment, and Completion in Developmental Education Sequences in Community Colleges."

16. Ibid., 11.

17. Ibid., 13.

18. Attewell, Heil, and Reisel, "Competing Explanations of Undergraduate Noncompletion." 915.

19. Eric Bettinger and Bridget Terry Long, "Remediation at the Community College: Student Participation and Outcomes," *New Directions for Community Colleges* 129, Spring (2005); Eric Bettinger and Bridget Terry Long, "Addressing the Needs of Under-Prepared Students in Higher Education: Does College Remediaion Work?" in *NBER Working Series Paper* (Cambridge, MA: National Bureau of Economic Research, 2005).

20. Bettinger and Long, "Addressing the Needs of Under-Prepared Students in Higher Education: Does College Remediaion Work?" 24.

21. Juan Carlos Calcagno and Bridget Terry Long, "The Impact of Postsecondary Remediation Using a Regression Discontinuity Approach: Addreessing Endogenous Sorting and Noncompliance," (New York, NY: National Center for Postsecondary Research, Teachers College, Columbia University, 2008).

22. Ibid., 3.

23. Paul Attewell et al., "New Evidence on College Remediation," Journal of Higher Education 77, no. 5 (2006).

24. Dolors Perin and Kerry Charron, "Can Community Colleges Protect Both Access and Standards? The Problem of Remediation," *Teachers College Record* 108, no. 3 (2006).

25. Quoting from another report: Katherine L. Hughes and Judith Scott-Clayton, "Assessing Developmental Assessment in Community Colleges," (New York: Community College Research Center, 2011), 9.

26. Ibid.

27. Ibid., 12.

28. Ibid., 37.

29. Clive Belfield and Thomas Bailey, "The Benefits of Attending Community College: A Review of the Evidence," *Community college Review* 39, no. 1 (2011).

30. ACT Inc., "Act National Curriculum Survey, 2009," (Iowa City, IA: ACT, Inc., 2009).

31. Ibid., 5.

32. Ibid., 7.

33. Norton Grubb and Rebecca Cox, "Pedagogical Alignment and Curricular Consistency: The Challenges for Developmental Education," *New Directions for Community Colleges* 129, no. Spring (2005).

34. Dolores Perin, "Facilitating Student Learning through Contextualization " in CCRC Brief No. 53, ed. Teachers College Community College Research Center, Columbia University (New York, NY: Community College Research Center, Teachers College, Columbia University, 2011).

35. Nikki Edgecombe, "Accelerating the Academic Achievement of Students Referred to Developmental Education," (New York, NY: Community College Research Center, Teachers College, Columbia University, 2011).

36. Davis Jenkins et al., "A Model for Accelerating Academic Success of Community College Remedial English Students: Is the Accelerated Learning Program (ALP) Effective and Affordable?," (New York: Community College Research Center, Teachers College, Columbia University, 2010).

37. Matt Zeidenberg, Sung-Woo Cho, and Davis Jenkins, "Washington State's Integrated Basic Education and Skills Training Program (I-BEST): New Evidence of Effectiveness," (New York, NY: Community College Research Center, Teachers College, Columbia University, 2010).

38. "Instructional Design Principles for Statway™," (Stanford, CA: The Carnegie Foundation for the Advancement of Teaching, 2010), 2. May be retrieved at www.carnegiefoundation.org/sites/default/files/statway-design-principles.pdf.

39. Peter Ewell, "Community College Bridges to Opportunity Initiative: Joint State Data Toolkit," (Austin, TX: Bridges to Opportunity Initiative and Community College Leadership Program, University of Texas at Austin, 2007).

40. Timothy Leinbach and Davis Jenkins, "Using Longitudinal Data to Increase Community College Student Success: A Guide to Measuring Milestone and Momentum Point Attainment," in *CCRC Research Tools* (New York, NY: Community College Research Center, Teachers College, Columbia University, 2008), 1.

41. Henry M. Levin and Juan Carlos Calcagno, "Remediation in the Community College: An Evaluator's Perspective," *Community College Review* 35, no. 3 (2008).

Chapter Three

Campus Context of Student Success

Although it varies from college to college, one does not typically see a significant amount of student interaction occurring outside of class on community college campuses. Students study in public areas between classes and mingle in groups at cafeteria tables. In the winter, they sit in their cars between classes, engines running to stay warm. For some it is a matter of listening to music or finding a quiet place to study, but for many it is a chance to nap because a typical day can be a continuum of work and school. Many a community college instructor who has taught at 8 a.m. will attest to the student, usually in the back row with a large cup of coffee, who just came off the night shift at work. The absence of social life on community college campuses contrasts starkly with the crowded pathways of public high schools and residential colleges and universities, where students socialize in groups and people recognize and greet each other even at a distance.

Part of the explanation for this is that community colleges offer classes nearly twenty-four hours a day. In addition, distance education classes now comprise a significant portion of the enrollment on many campuses. Community colleges are alive at night, with full parking lots and lights on in many classrooms. The evening college is also the part-time college, made up largely of adult learners taking classes from part-time faculty. While students and adjunct faculty toil away late into the evening, most full-time faculty, staff, and administrators have gone home long before. While evidence is inconclusive about the efficacy of adjuncts, their work is framed by limitations that have implications for student success.[1] For example, adjunct faculty teach in relative isolation because many are on campus only during the evening hours. Most have limited voice mail and office access on campus, and they often hold more than one job.

In June 2008, an article in the Atlantic Monthly written by Professor X, a community college adjunct professor, described his experience teaching English 102 to students in an evening class.[2] Professor X was bothered by the fact that his students were unprepared for college work and that, in the end, it was the grade he gave to these students that would have a bearing on their chances of success. As he described it, "[f]or I, who teach these low-level, must-pass, no-multiple-choice-test classes, am the one who ultimately delivers the news to those unfit for college: that they lack the most-basic skills and have no sense of the volume of work required...I am the man who has to lower the hammer."[3] As desirable as it is to argue that he is wrong and that all of his students could succeed under the right conditions, those perfect conditions do not exist. Community colleges are structured so that high stakes situations—where students need academic and emotional support in order to succeed—often unfold under conditions when the least support is available for either instructors or students.

Whether they attend during the day, evening or both, community college students spend little time on campus. Although most community colleges offer club and student activities to engage students, CCSSE (Community College Survey of Student Engagement) results from the 2011 cohort suggest that as few as 18 percent of students participate in college-sponsored activities such as organizations, campus publications, student government, and sports. In general, community college students move between class, work, and home with little time for social activities. Does it matter? Does engagement in campus life contribute to student success? What does research tell us that will strengthen community college practice in this area?

ACADEMIC AND SOCIAL INTEGRATION

Community colleges offer access to students with wide ranging goals through an infrastructure that supports part-time attendance and opportunities to attend class during the day, evening, or weekend. As a result, they are popular with older as well as younger students who need to limit their living expenses by staying close to home for college. Community college students are described in the literature as "nontraditional" because on average they are older than students at a four-year colleges and universities. They also tend to be more racially and ethnically diverse; and they are more likely to be financially independent, often with dependents of their own.

Part-time students currently make up 59 percent[4] of the credit headcount enrollment at community colleges. Part-time enrollment climbed rapidly during the 1970s with one out of two (47 percent) students enrolled part-time in 1970 compared to six out of ten (61 percent) in 1980.[5] Cohen and Brawer attribute this change to the number of students combining work and study and to an increase in the number of women attending college. It is also worth noting that much of the growth in part-time enrollment occurred during a decade when enrollments nearly doubled. Increased accessibility to college combined with the declining value of the high school diploma and availability of the GI Bill for returning Vietnam veterans, made community colleges the postsecondary institution of choice for adult learners.[6]

While geographic proximity and flexibility are important factors contributing to the growth of community colleges, they create structural challenges for students. Age is a risk factor with respect to college completion as many adult learners attend college with short-term goals related to workforce skills in contrast to completing degrees or transfer. Family background is also a risk factor. Research suggests that first-generation students have a significantly greater risk of dropping out of college. One study found that students whose parents had not attended college were 8.5 times more likely to drop out, and that the higher odds of dropping out persisted beyond the first year.[7]

Tinto's theory of academic and social integration has been highly influential in the postsecondary literature in shaping our knowledge of the process through which students disengage from college.[8] The decision to leave college is, after all, not spontaneous, but develops incrementally over time. At community colleges, where students do not need to relocate, forfeit money, or to discuss a withdrawal decision with staff, withdrawing from classes can seem inconsequential—at least from a student perspective. The decision to drop out of college can be completely invisible to a student who withdraws from classes with plans to reenroll in the future. Not surprisingly, "stop-out," is a strong predictor of dropout.[9]

Tinto uses sociological theory to examine the process through which students become part of the college culture. The transformation from high school to college student moves through three stages. The first phase is separation from communities of the past. For students leaving home to attend college, this can be separation that is reinforced by geography. In this phase, community college students are disadvantaged, because, although the transition to college is less stressful because they are not leaving home, it is also less rewarding in that many aspects of their lives remain unchanged. Thus, indicates Tinto, "the ironic situation [is] that, though they may find the task of persistence initially easier, it may be measurably more difficult over the long run."[10]

The second phase is the transition phase in which a high school graduate learns how to be a college student. During this phase, students must become socialized to accept the norms and values of their new environment. Student orientation and student success courses are aimed at helping students during this phase. The final phase is "incorporation into the society of the college." Although some students easily navigate this phase—they are the ones participating in student government, in the student newspaper, working on campus, or carrying more than thirty earned credits on their transcripts—they represent a only a small subset of students at community colleges.

Tinto uses this phased entry model of transition to college as a basis for exploring why some students fail to make the transition. What are the causes for departure before reaching the third phase? He draws on Emile Durkheim's theory of suicide to understand how and why this might happen.[11] One form of suicide is linked to insufficient integration of individuals into society. The failure to experience a sense of membership results from misalignment between the individual's norms, beliefs, and values and those of community members. For students, college life is defined by two systems: the academic system and the social system. A student's inability to integrate into campus life results from a lack of alignment into one or both of these systems.

Tinto's work has been subjected to extensive debate and testing. In general, the results have been mixed in terms of the impact of academic integration on student departure.[12] Researchers have argued that the theory needs to be reformulated for two-year and commuter institutions. One problem is that organized social activities (including clubs, organizations, or sports teams) are limited in number on community college campuses. But, social integration can also include peer friendships on campus and relationships with faculty and staff outside of class. Finding little attention in the research to social integration on commuter campuses, Bean and Metzner parceled out this factor in their model of nontraditional undergraduate student attrition.[13]

Tinto also observed that "a potentially large number of students will choose to depart from an institution because they have come to see that further participation in the institution no longer serves their best interests. In some cases this may reflect differences in goals. In others, it may reflect the absence of sufficient commitment to pursue specific goals."[14] By design, the emphasis on accessibility has led community colleges to minimize constraints that might tie students to campus. Last minute deadlines, low cost, part-time attendance, and late withdrawal dates work to send students the message that commitment is not a requirement of the college. Furthermore, students' goals are expected to change, because community colleges are a springboard rather than a final destination.

Community colleges are extraordinarily porous. Students flow in and out easily and a terminology has developed to describer behaviors that are commonplace. "Stop-outs" are students who do not appear in institutional records for a period of time even though they eventually return and continue working toward a degree. Students are also prone to "swirling,"—a term attributed to Cliff Adelman based on his findings that multi-institutional attendance is now commonplace.[15] Students take courses at various institutions (sometimes appearing to be a stop-out or dropout) like consumers in a shopping mall carrying multiple shopping bags. These behaviors create problems for researchers seeking to understand student outcomes. Are swirlers still students? Did they leave college permanently? It is almost impossible to understand why certain forms of student behavior happen if we cannot figure out what the behavior is in the first place.

Tinto's theory has the potential to provide insight into why students stay in college. Is it possible that finding ways to integrate students into campus life might increase their chances of staying? How can a college encourage engagement in campus life so that students perceive faculty and coursework as supporting their goals, and social integration as a means through which they can form supportive bonds with other students at the institution?

In her ethnographic study of community college classrooms, Cox brought together results from research studies involving classroom observations and interviews with faculty and students.[16] She found that students bring strong expectations about the roles of college instructors and students to the classroom, and that these expectations were often out of alignment with those of instructors. The result was that both students and faculty perceived each other as failing to meet their expectations, which served to prevent "learners from the kind of active engagement in coursework that would be needed for them to succeed."[17]

Some community college instructors in her study "narrowed the distance between themselves and their students."[18] As described by Cox, "[F]rom the start of the semester, Beth and Julie actively reached out to students, establishing encouraging relationships and fostering a comfortable classroom atmosphere. In some instances, they engaged in practices not standard in postsecondary contexts such as calling students who missed class, or sending spontaneous e-mail messages to individual students from week to week."[19] Based on these findings, a viable approach to improving student success might be to bring instructors and students closer together through instructor efforts to nurture academic engagement in students.

Through interviews with 238 community college students, Deil-Amen found that connections with peer and faculty occurring at the classroom level were highly important to students.[20] Approximately three-quarters of the students in her study described the "support and approachability of teachers and student peers in classrooms as fundamental to their feelings of comfort in college."[21] She found that colleges could proactively create socially integrative moments for students by focusing on how they could be created inside classrooms since they are not likely to occur outside of class for most students.

Community colleges have developed tools to measure and analyze the extent to which students are integrated into campus life. How often do they interact with instructors and other students? How welcome do they feel? What are their needs, and how willing are they to find support on campus? In the next section I review some of the surveys that provide this information at the campus level.

MEASURING STUDENT ENGAGEMENT

While four-year colleges and universities have been measuring the academic and social experiences of their first-year students for decades, community colleges are relative newcomers to this practice. Several reasons account for the late arrival. Primary among them is the culture of the open door college. As observed earlier, along with easy entry comes a tacit acceptance of easy exit. Community colleges have pursued a strategy of integration into the larger community, rather than remaining distinct from it. Accordingly, the notion of students becoming socialized by the institution and becoming part of its unique culture has not been a high priority. Second, there are methodological challenges to surveying students and identifying them as a specific "cohort" because of the diversity of academic needs and goals. Third, the instruments that have been used extensively by four-year colleges and universities, in particular the CIRP Freshman Survey[22] and National Survey of Student Engagement (NSSE),[23] did not lend themselves to a community college setting, which meant that appropriate instruments were not available until the past decade.

Fortunately times have changed, and community colleges are now able to survey and gather data from students on their social and academic experiences. Three surveys provide important insights into campus life for community college leaders, staff and researchers.

Community College Survey of Student Engagement (CCSSE)

The CCSSE survey is based on the National Survey of Student Engagement (NSSE) which was piloted in 1999. While NSSE is headquartered at Indiana University, CCSSE is headquartered at the University of Texas. First administered in 2001, by spring 2011 CCSSE had grown to a volume of 443,818 useable surveys returned nationwide on 699 campuses.[24]

CCSSE is theoretically and empirically grounded in higher education research on student learning and engagement. Specifically, research conducted by Pascarella, Terenzini, and Tinto provides the foundation upon which the survey is built.[25] A 1984 National Institute of Education report titled "Involvement in Learning" and seven principles put forth by Chickering and Gamson informs many the questions asked in the survey.[26]

The CCSSE is fundamentally concerned with a model of active learning which includes frequent interaction between students and teachers, discussion and feedback, and proactive learning. It also seeks information about institutional structures relating to student services and academic support.

Respondents are asked to indicate the extent of their involvement in a range of college services, such as: tutoring, developmental education, learning communities, and orientation programs. They must indicate both the scope of their involvement in these activities and their rating of the importance of each. The survey also asks students to report on how many hours each week are spent in various school and nonschool activities. These include reading, writing papers, studying, working, and caring for dependents.

The sampling technique for this survey involves randomly selecting ten percent of credit students. The students are selected by a random sampling of classrooms. Surveys are conducted by college faculty or staff during the middle of the spring semester. Students may not take the survey twice. In order to adjust for a higher likelihood of full-time students being selected for the survey, results are weighted according the actual proportion of full-time students at the college.

The responses to CCSSE survey questions are scaled to construct five benchmarks:

- Active and Collaborative Learning
- Student Effort
- Academic Challenge
- Student-Faculty Interaction
- Support for Learners

Each benchmark is normed using three years of CCSSE data. The results are presented to participating colleges in a report which includes item frequencies and means as well as benchmarks. The benchmarks allow colleges to compare their results with other colleges. It is possible to compare against a national sample as well as a consortium of institutions, which is a pre-determined subset. The report allows colleges to see not only how they differ from the norm, but the specific items on which their results differ statistically from the comparison group. This makes it possible for a college to identify its strengths and weaknesses.

In 2006, a validation study was conducted to determine how well the survey instrument predicted student outcomes.[27] The results of this study indicated that the Active and Collaborative Learning benchmark effectively predicted persistence while the Academic Challenge benchmark predicted academic outcomes only. Not surprisingly, Support for Learners had the strongest impact on persistence, but did not show effects for academic outcomes. Student-Faculty Interaction and Student Effort revealed minimal effects which are thought to reflect the limited contact that community college students have with instructors and one other.

The Survey of Entering Student Engagement (SENSE)

SENSE was developed in partnership with CCSSE in an effort to focus on the early experiences of college students. Since CCSSE is administered in the spring, it has the disadvantage of providing little information about the experiences of students who disengage from college. To learn more about students who do not become integrated into the social and academic life of college, the SENSE survey is conducted during the fourth and fifth weeks of the fall semester. Its aim is to provide feedback to colleges on student "behaviors in the earliest weeks of college and the institutional practices that affect students during this critical time" (http://www.ccsse.org/sense/about-survey/index.cfm). SENSE is a smaller and newer survey than CCSSE, and was first conducted in fall 2009. The fall 2010 SENSE involved 75,000 students attending 172 community and technical colleges in 35 states, the District of Columbia, and the Mariana Islands. SENSE benchmarks are based on the 2009 and 2010 administrations, bringing the total number surveys collected to 129,207.[28]

SENSE is headquartered at the University of Texas, Austin and the survey is administered in roughly the same way as CCSSE. The major difference is that SENSE is keyed to randomized selection of class sections and draws only on courses that are likely to be taken by entry-level college students. These courses include developmental English and mathematics (but not English as a Second Language), first-year English and first-year mathematics. Students may not take the survey twice. The results of the survey distinguish between those students who are new (in their first semester at the college) and those who are continuing. Similar to CCSSE, data are weighted to account for the over-sampling of full-time students.

The responses to survey questions are scaled into six benchmarks:

* Early Connections
* High Expectations and Aspirations
* Clear Academic Plan and Pathway
* Effective Track to College Readiness
* Engaged Learning
* Academic and Social Support Network

This survey captures the challenges faced by new students on community college campuses. Nationally, only about 24 percent of students surveyed responded that a particular person at their college had been assigned to them for advising and assistance. Furthermore, 39 percent of respondents disagreed or strongly disagreed that a college staff member had helped them determine their eligibility for financial aid. Approximately one-quarter of the students had failed to turn in an assignment within the first five weeks of school, nearly a third had already handed an assignment in late, and nearly half had not done required reading for a course.[29]

Noel-Levitz College Student Inventory (CSI)

The Noel-Levitz CSI measures the degree to which students are at risk of dropping out of college. The survey is primarily designed for use by counselors and advisors. There are three versions of the survey enabling it to be conducted either on paper or online. The online version was designed with adult and community college students in mind, while the written forms were designed for a traditionally aged, residential four-year college population.

  The Noel-Levitz CSI is made up of one hundred items which are scaled to form thirteen individual scales and four summary scales (combinations of items in the individual scales). The individual scales are grouped in three areas: Academic Motivation, General Coping, and Receptivity to Support.[30] The scales themselves focus on students' self-assessment in areas such as reading, writing and mathematics preparation, and study habits; the use of technology; the need for financial, academic, and career planning; and financial security. The four summary scales are Overall Risk, Acknowledged Academic Needs, Apprehension Index, and Receptivity Index. The results are organized into specialized reports for students, counselors, and administrators as well as into raw data that can be downloaded by institutional researchers. Results are presented through an online dashboard, which allows the user to organize and sort information so that it is easy to identify students who need support.

The CSI is administered early in the semester when students are new to a college. Because the CSI comes with a robust online reporting system and easy access to raw data, it can be used in two ways: 1) to capture information about students and the degree to which they are at risk of dropout at a time when it is still possible to intervene and 2) to analyze the efficacy of interventions through information that can help control for a variety of factors that help and hinder student progress. Research validating the CSI for use with community college populations is limited. For this reason, it is advisable to administer a pilot and use the data to predict student success before using it in a situation in which an intervention is attempted. This will provide a baseline understanding of the validity of the CSI in predicting student outcomes at a specific institution.

ENHANCING SOCIAL AND ACADEMIC INTEGRATION

Community colleges do not face a wide range of options when it comes to increasing academic and social integration. Students minimize their time on campus because they have jobs, families, and friendships outside of college that require time and attention. Arguably, some have chosen the community college as a place to enroll precisely because they want to attend a college that minimizes time to degree. What students do not realize, however, is that bonds with instructors and peers are instrumental because they increase the likelihood of persistence and, ultimately, of obtaining a degree.

In reality, community colleges have roughly six to eight weeks to engage first-time students. First impressions matter. According to the data generated by colleges in the Achieving the Dream database, 14 percent of students earn no credits during their first semester.[31] Black students are the most likely subgroup to end the semester with no credits (18 percent), Hispanic students rank second (15 percent), and 12 percent of white students finish with no credits. Part-time students are much more likely to be zero credit earners (17 percent) than full-time students (9 percent percent). Persistence into the next semester is unlikely for zero credit earners, as only 15 percent return for a second semester compared with 74 percent of students who earned credits.

Community colleges are actively involved in developing First-year Experience strategies to engage students. Examples of efforts being made on community college campuses to increase student engagement include the following:

Learning Communities. Learning communities take a variety of forms, but the underlying premise is that a group of students takes two or more courses together and instructors in those courses work as a team to design and deliver the curriculum. Although other models exist, learning communities generally work in linked courses with participation lasting over the course of one semester. Community colleges have engaged in a variety of practices with regard to the selection of courses that are linked and how those connections are made. For example, at LaGuardia Community College in Queens, New York, learning communities are part of a First Year Academy. First Year Academies are offered in Business and Technology, Allied Health, and Liberal Arts. Each academy has at least one basic skills course (if needed), a seminar for first year students, an introductory course in their major, and a Studio Hour where students learn how to build an e-portfolio. Kingsborough Community College offers a range of options for learning communities, including Opening Doors Learning Communities, comprising as many as thirty-three cohorts each semester of up to twenty-five students taking block programs of linked courses: English, the Freshman Seminar, and a General Education Discipline course. Kingsborough also offers learning communities in English as a Second Language and Advanced Learning Communities for students in their second semester.

Best practices associated with learning communities focus on developing an integrated and holistic learning experience for students based on the belief that "[s]tudents persist in their studies if the learning they experience is meaningful, deeply engaging, and relevant to their lives."[32] For example, when instructors develop shared assignments, it not only relieves the pressure of competing academic demands on students (i.e., two different papers due on the same day), but demonstrates connections between subject areas so that students understand academic skill development as a comprehensive process.

When a true community of learners emerges, students and instructors work as a team. Instructors visit each other's classrooms and work on integrating curriculum. This enables them to expand upon the topics and concepts presented in the learning community from unique disciplinary perspectives while at the same time helping students forge connections in their knowledge and understanding of subjects. Connectivity between instructors also makes it easier to identify students who are having difficulty in more than one subject area and to match students having difficulty with the services that will help them.

A downside of learning communities is that they are difficult to implement, particularly with respect to recruiting faculty.[33] They depend on flexible systems in course scheduling, registration, advising, and faculty workload. Course schedules are typically built as much as a year in advance, and often rely on "rolling" information from a previous semester. Structures of this type mean that when a decision to form a learning community comes after the course schedule has been created, instructor workloads must be rearranged or new instructors added. If learning communities are planned in advance of schedule building, there must still be a reallocation of course sections to create learning communities. Needless to say, carrying this off requires careful coordination and communication among academic departments.

The social dynamics among students in learning communities remain largely unexplored. While it has been assumed that community college students are not interested in social connections on campus, learning communities challenge this assumption. In the Visher et al. 2010 report, which is part of the National Center for Postsecondary Research's Learning Communities Demonstration project, most students reported that being part of a learning community "helped them feel more comfortable in the classroom and more supported by—and supportive of—their fellow students."[34] Students and instructors participating in learning communities in the study reported a stronger sense of accountability among students and increased comfort levels in contributing to classroom discussion.

The literature suggests that single semester learning communities at community colleges are a relatively high cost intervention, leading to modest short-term effects. However, the popularity of learning communities among instructors teaching in them and the anecdotal information about the benefits of integrative and active, collaborative learning suggest that much remains to be learned. It is also interesting to contemplate whether the social dynamics described by Visher et al. might be linked to active and collaborative learning rather than learning communities. If this is the case, it is possible that the value of learning communities is their capacity to reduce the isolation of faculty, bring about a strengthened ability to develop active, collaborative pedagogical styles.

Student Orientation and Success Courses

Student success courses are another promising approach to helping students build the skills and connections that will help them to be successful in college. These classes are provided early in the college experience, generally during the first semester of enrollment. Typically, the content emphasis of student success courses is fourfold: to introduce students to campus resources; to give them an opportunity to get to know student peers and instructors; to clarify aspirations; and to develop academic and life management skills. Durham Technical Community College in North Carolina has implemented a college success course through Achieving the Dream in which instruction is provided in study skills and academic planning. The retention rate of students participating in the course is 20 percent higher than students who did not enroll in the course.

There are difficulties in evaluating the efficacy of student success courses at community colleges because there is so much variation in their design and because there can be a strong self-selection bias influencing student participation. With respect to delivery, curricula vary considerably from college to college and it is not possible to determine the extent to which course content focused on study skills, academic planning and financial aid actually helped students. Practitioners have little choice, therefore, but to adopt the perspective that student success courses offer colleges an opportunity to convey to students the information that research suggests is associated with college success. Karp's research on nonacademic supports for student success provides some guidance.[35] Social relationships created on campus were found to clarify career and educational aspirations, to develop college "know-how," and to make college life easier to navigate.

Reform Advising Processes

The concept of case management has been borrowed from social service organizations and used in campus efforts to redesign academic advising. The premise is that students are assigned to case managers (counselors or advisors, for example) who are responsible for moving individuals systematically toward a predefined set of outcomes. Case management has been implemented by colleges through specialized grant programs such as the Student Support Services (TRIO), but is now making its way into the mainstream of college services. It is possible that in order to scale up these kinds of services, community colleges will need to assign the management aspect to electronic resources such as e-portfolios. Students can be provided with assessment templates to complete which can be archived electronically and retrieved as necessary by personnel in support services.

The LifeMap system at Valencia College has received national attention for its innovative approach to providing students with a system of stages through which they can independently pursue educational and career goals. It is described as: "a student's guide to figuring out 'what to do when' in order to complete career and educational goals. LifeMap links all of the components of Valencia (faculty, staff, courses, technology, programs, services) into a personal itinerary to help students succeed in their college experience."[36] The program consists of five LifeMap stages: college transition; introduction to college; progression to degree; graduation transition; and lifelong learning. Each of these stages relates to a specified range of credits earned by the student. The college uses a variety of assessments to help students in planning, and to provide them with indicators that indicate whether they are meeting expectations at each stage.

The costs and challenges of implementing a system of case management appear to vary and are not well known. A caseload assigned to a specific individual is beyond the means of the typical community college, since counselor caseloads typically number in the thousands.[37] However, creative uses of technology may bring customization of student support services within reach. For example, if a student is able to archive the results of a wide range of assessments, including everything from placement tests to research papers, then a more sophisticated approach to diagnosing student challenges and recommending interventions may emerge.

Financial Supports

Limited income is a problem confronting many community college students with implications for social and academic integration. The most damaging effect of low income is that students may have to attend college part-time or intermittently to save enough money to cover their college and living expenses. Limited income also has a bearing on the stress levels of students because they have less time to study and are constantly juggling multiple responsibilities including work and college. If their academic experience is limited, community college students are apt to be working for low wages which means that they will need to work longer hours to earn enough money to stay in college. The stakes increase as students become older, since middle-aged students will have substantially less time to accrue the increased lifetime earnings that were the motivation to attend college.

Efforts to help low income students pursuing college degrees have come primarily in the form of student aid programs at both the federal and state levels. Since community college students are disproportionately part-time and tuition is relatively low, students have not received proportional amounts of federal aid in comparison to other sectors of higher education.[38] The College Cost Reduction and Affordability Act of 2007 lifted caps linking the size of the Pell grant to a proportion of college tuition, thereby increasing access to Pell grants for community college students. In 2010–2011, 36.5 percent of Pell grant recipients attended community colleges.[39] In the past few years government agencies report there have been substantial increases in Pell spending overall resulting in gains for community colleges. Between 2009–2010 and 2010–2011 the proportion of community college students receiving Pell grants increased by 21 percent, with the Pell allocation to them increasing by 19 percent.[40]

The picture is not entirely rosy. Pell grants cover as little as 29 percent of tuition, room and board for students at public two-year colleges.[41] Studies show that community college students are less likely to access aid and more likely to have inadequate information about aid than undergraduates starting at four-year colleges and universities. Findings from a Public Agenda study indicate that 72 percent of high school graduates who either did not attend college or left college early were unable to "give even a general definition" of the FAFSA form which is the first step toward obtaining government financial aid.[42] Aside from finding the system confusing and being skeptical about borrowing money for college, survey and focus group respondents in multiple studies did not see full-time study as an option.[43]

Foundations are starting to tackle the issue of limited personal funds through scholarships and emergency aid as a mechanism for keeping students in college. Dreamkeepers is a program of Scholarship America working with thirty-one community colleges nationwide to provide students with financial assistance. This scholarship fund is designed to help students remain in college even when they are confronted by a financial emergency. College staff are trained to provide services, and grants are made available to help students get through the financial emergency, as well as to access additional support through student services. Similar to other financial programs, Dreamkeepers is interested in promoting financial literacy, and to this end offers a web portal designed to help students build long-term money management skills.

CONCLUSION

If community colleges are to move toward a paradigm of student success, then processes through which students form academic and social bonds within institutions need to be better understood. When community college graduates reflect on their successes, they typically describe pivotal moments in their academic careers in terms of people who supported them. Often it is a connection with a particular instructor, counselor, or advisor at the college. For others, it is a group such a club or as Phi Theta Kappa. In any event, it is hard to imagine a student reaching graduation without personal connections on campus. By offering little in the way of opportunities to new students to develop social bonds within the campus community, community colleges fail to acknowledge the importance of integration into campus life related by those who have achieved success.

The characteristics of community college students make it all the more important that colleges become proactive in reaching out to students. Students who are part-time, commuting, weighed down with the demands of adult life, or first-generation college attendees need the social capital that can be provided by college faculty, staff, and peers. Thoughtfully developed social networks are the kind of safety net students need to reduce the likelihood that they will leave college early.

It is not simply that students lead challenging lives, however. Nationally, two-thirds of community college faculty are part-time instructors. Students and instructors are coming together primarily in the context of the classroom, with neither spending much time on campus. Adjunct faculty are a staple at community colleges which, from a strictly educational standpoint, should not adversely impact students. Adjunct faculty in career programs have substantial practical experience, which is critical to the success of students in preparing for and finding jobs. For example, in culinary arts, finding an excellent baker from the community to teach baking may provide much more value to students than having the course taught by a chef with a different specialty.

Despite these positives, however, a culture of part-time presence and transience has serious implications for the ability of institutions to strengthen cultural connections with students. Instructors divide teaching responsibilities among multiple institutions and have limited contact with students at any one of them. By implication, extra effort is required to communicate and instill institutional core values in part-time faculty.

MeVida Burrus, a graduate of Oakland Community College in Michigan, provided a wonderful example of the importance of academic and social integration in her keynote speech at the 2012 D.R.E.A.M. Institute. MeVida, despite being active in Phi Theta Kappa and other campus groups, nearly missed the graduation deadline at her college because she had no idea that an application was part of the process. "It wasn't that the information wasn't communicated. I saw it" she explained; it just did not grab her attention. MeVida believes that "people perish for lack of knowledge" and in response to her experience with the graduation deadline, organized a Commit to Complete rally through Phi Theta Kappa.

"Commit to Complete" is Phi Theta Kappa's contribution to the Community College Completion Challenge (C4), which is a joint venture among six national community college organizations to produce five million more Associate degree and certificate holders by 2020. The Phi Theta Kappa students at Oakland titled their rally "OCC: Overcome + Commitment = Complete" and, with help from student services offices, the president's office, local businesses, and others they were able to hold an event that connected students with the information they need from enrollment to graduation. By the end of the rally, Oakland Community College had 250 students who signed a commitment to graduate, and the list continues to grow.

NOTES

1. Norton Grubb, "Learning and Earning in the Middle: The Economic Benefits of Sub-Baccalaureate Education," (New York, NY: Community College Research Center, Teachers College, Columbia University, 1999).

2. Professor X, "In the Basement of the Ivory Tower," *The Atlantic*, June 2008.

3. Ibid.

4. U.S. Department of Education, National Center for Education Statistics, "Condition of Education," (Washginton, DC: National Center for Education Statistics, 2011), Table 201.

5. Arthur M. Cohen and Florence B. Brawer, *The American Community College, Fourth Edition* (San Francisco: Jossey-Bass, 2003), 41.

6. Steven Brint and Jerome Karabel, *The Diverted Dream: Community Colleges and the Promise of Educational Opportunity in America, 1900 - 1985* (New York: Oxford University Press, 1989); Kevin J. Dougherty, *The Contradictory College: The Conflicting Origins, Impacts, and Futures of the Community Colleges* (Albany, NY: State University of New York Press, 1994).

7. Terry T. Ishitani, "Studying Attrition and Degree Completion Behavior among First-Generation College Students in the United States," *Journal of Higher Education* 77, no. 5 (2006).

8. Vincent Tinto, "Dropout from Higher Education: A Theoretical Synthesis of Recent Research," *Review of Educational Research* 45 (1975); Vincent Tinto, *Leaving College: Rethinking the Causes and Cures of Student Attrition*, Second Edition (Chicago: University of Chicago Press, 1993).

9. Clifford Adelman, "Answers in the Toolbox: Academic Intensity, Attendance Patterns, and Bachelor's Degree Attainment," (Washington, DC.: U.S. Department of Education, 1999).

10. Vincent Tinto, *Leaving College: Rethinking the Causes and Cures of Student Attrition*, 96.

11. Emile Durkheim, *Suicide*, trans. J. A. Spaulding and G. Simpson (Glencoe, NY: The Free Press, 1951).

12. John M. Braxton and Leigh A. Lien, "The Viability of Academic Integration as a Central Construct in Tinto's Interactionist Theory of College Student Departure," in *Reworking the Student Departure Puzzle*, ed. John M. Braxton (Nashville, TN: Vanderbilt University Press, 2000).

13. John P. Bean and Barbara S. Metzner, "A Conceptual Model of Nontraditional Undergraduate Student Attrition," *Review of Educational Research* 55, no. 4 (1985).

14. Tinto, *Leaving College: Rethinking the Causes and Cures of Student Attrition*, 142.

15. Clifford Adelman, "The Toolbox Revisited: Paths to Degree Completion from High School through College," (Washington, DC: U.S. Department of Education, 2006).

16. Rebecca D. Cox, *The College Fear Factor: How Students and Professors Misunderstand One Another* (Cambridge, MA: Harvard University Press, 2009).

17. Ibid., 158.

18. Ibid., 128.

19. Ibid., 129.

20. Regina Deil-Amen, "Socio-Academic Integrative Moments: Rethinking Academic and Social Integration among Two-Year College Students in Career-Related Programs," *The Journal of Higher Education* 82, no. 1 (2011).

21. Ibid., 63.

22. As of the time of writing, more information about the CIRP Freshman Survey can be obtained at http://www.heri.ucla.edu/herisurveys.php.

23. As of the time of writing, more information about the NSSE survey can be obtained at http://www.nsse.iub.edu.

24. Obtained from http://www.ccsse.org.

25. Tinto, *Leaving College: Rethinking the Causes and Cures of Student Attrition*; Ernest Pascarella and Patrick Terenzini, *How College Affects Students* (San Francisco: Jossey-Bass, 1991).

26. Study Group on the Conditions of Excellence in American Higher Education, "Involvement in Learning: Realizing the Potential of American Higher Education," (Washington, DC: National Institute of Education, 1884); Arthur W. Chickering, Zelda F. Gamson, and Susan J. Poulsen, *Seven Principles for Good Practice in Undergraduate Education* (Racine, WI: Johnson Foundation, 1987).

27. Kay M. McClenney and C. Nathan Marti, "Exploring Relationships between Student Engagement and Student Outcomes in Community Colleges: Report on Validation Research," (Austin, TX: Community College Survey of Student Engagement at the Community College Leadership Program, The University of Texas at Austin, December 2006).

28. As of the time of writing, more information about the SENSE survey can be obtained at http://www.ccsse.org/sense/survey/overview.cfm.

29. Information published on the CCSSE website: http://www.ccsse.org/sense/survey/survey.cfm.

30. Information published on the Noel-Levitz website: http://www.noellevitz.com/student-retention-solutions/retention-management-system/college-student-inventory.

31. Achieving the Dream, "Students Earning Zero Credits," in *Data Notes* (Achieving the Dream, 2008).

32. Emily Lardner and Gillies Malnarich, "A New Era in Learning-Community Work: Why the Pedagogy of Intentional Integration Matters," *Change Magazine*, no. July–August (2008).

33. Mary G. Visher et al., "Scaling up Learning Communities: The Experience of Six Community Colleges," (New York: National Center for Postsecondary Research, 2010).

34. Ibid., 76.

35. Melinda Mechur Karp, "Toward a New Understanding of Non-Academic Student Support: Four Mechanisms Encouraging Positive Student Outcomes in the Community College," (New York,: Teachers College, Columbia University, 2011).

36. As of the time of writing, more information about the Valencia's LifeMap system can be obtained at http http://valenciacollege.edu/lifemap.

37. W. Norton Grubb, ""Like, What Do I Do Now?": The Dilemmas of Guidance Counseling," in *Defending the Community College Equity Agenda*, ed. Thomas R. Bailey and Vanessa Smith Morest (Baltimore: Johns Hopkins University Press, 2006).

38. Cohen and Brawer, *The American Community College, Fourth Edition*, 211.

39. David S. Baime and Christopher M. Mullin, "Promoting Educational Opportunity: The Pell Grant Program at Community Colleges," (American Association of Community Colleges, July 2011), 11.

40. Ibid., 11.

41. V. Orozco and L. Mayo, "Keeping Students Enrolled: How Community Colleges Are Boosting Financial Resources for Their Students," (New York: Demos, January 2011).

42. Jean Johnson and Jon Rochkind, "With Their Whole Lives Ahead of Them: Myths and Realities About Why So Many Students Fail to Finish College," (New York: Public Agenda), 16.

43. Ibid., 20.

Chapter Four

Learning to Work, Working to Learn

For most students, regardless of whether they are attending a two-year or four-year college, pursuing a postsecondary degree is fundamentally an economic decision. In many countries, the timing of leaving school to enter the workforce is determined on the basis of test performance; by the age of sixteen students may already know the pathway they will take. In the United States, we are not nearly as prescriptive, and the relationship between school and work remains vague. There are potential benefits to this approach, which emphasizes independence and perseverance, but there are also pitfalls. Our higher education system is characterized by second or third chances, flexibility, and few explicit constraints. The downside of this system is that students must make many choices along the way. Often these choices are made on the basis of partial or inaccurate information.

A recent analysis yielded results that have been especially troubling to researchers and policy makers. Researchers were able to compare expectations for college completion in a sample of eighth grade students with their educational attainment twelve years later. They found that "whereas two-thirds of all eighth graders in the United States expected to complete a four-year degree, 12 years later less than one-third actually had done so."[1] Not surprisingly, socioeconomic status is a strong predictor of educational outcomes. Students coming from high socioeconomic status (SES) families were eight times more likely to complete college than lower SES students; a graduation rate of 60 percent for one group compared to 7 percent for the other.[2] When it comes to educational decision making, low SES students are at a disadvantage because of the heavy reliance placed by our system on ability to access information.[3]

At community colleges, students are handed course catalogs the size of telephone books with hundreds of options. Understanding how those options feed into careers is an overwhelming task for many students. There is an irony in our well-meaning desire to present students with a multitude of options. Too much information, but not enough guidance is not in the best interest of learners. In chapters 2 and 3, I reviewed some of the risk factors confronting community college students, which include weak reading skills and a system that provides little opportunity for early bonding experiences with faculty and staff. Yet, despite this scenario, we expect students to formulate career goals and workable educational plans. Instead of taking advantage of the vast array of options available to them, many students get lost in the system. In an effort to encourage transfer and long-term educational goals, community colleges have marginalized and underemphasized one of their most powerful resources: career and technical education (CTE).

CAREER AND TECHNICAL EDUCATION

Community colleges offer a wide range of occupational programs to students. These programs not only cover a broad variety of occupational fields, but are taught in multiple modalities making it possible for students to enroll in everything from workshops to degree programs. In 2009–2010, occupational degrees made up 59 percent of the Associate degrees granted in the United States and 64 percent of Associate degree enrollments.[4] Compared with academic programs, CTE Associate degree programs serve higher proportions of first generation college students (41 percent versus 36 percent), adults 25 or older (37 percent versus 25 percent), and students who have worked full-time (41 percent versus 35 percent).[5]

As table 4.1 shows, the largest numbers of degrees are granted in health and business fields. Community colleges also offer short-term certificates, most of which are less than two years in length. Certificates, like degrees, are well represented in fields such as health, business, mechanics, and culinary arts. Community colleges play a critical role in training first responders in occupations such as criminal justice, Emergency Medical Technician, practitioner nursing, and firefighting. They are also responsible for training many workers in service industries such as hospitality, culinary arts, early childhood education, and customer service. Whether one is on a movie set, checking into a hotel, or dropping off a child at daycare, there is a good chance that many of the employees performing the frontline work will have obtained some of their skills at a community college.

Career and technical education has been limited by its image which is rooted in its origins in vocational education. Vocational education was formalized during the Progressive Era with the passage of the Smith Hughes Act in 1917, at which time students of lower socioeconomic status were taught trade skills—working with metal and wood, sewing, and agriculture.

Table 4.1 Associate Degrees Conferred in the United States by Ten Largest
Degree Fields of Study

Degree Field of Study	Associate Degrees	Percent
1. Health professions and related programs	177,686	20.9%
2. Business	133,371	15.7%
3. Homeland security, law enforcement, firefighting, and related protective services	37,260	4.4%
4. Computer and information sciences	32,466	3.8%
5. Engineering technologies and engineering-related fields (Excluding "Construction trades" and "Mechanic and repair technologies/technicians")	31,850	3.7%
6. Education	17,048	2.0%
7. Mechanic and repair technologies/technicians	16,305	1.9%
8. Legal professions and studies	10,003	1.2%
9. Family and consumer sciences/human sciences	9,573	1.1%
10. Agriculture and natural resources	5,894	0.7%
Source: U.S. Department of Education, 2011, table 298.		

Trade skills became part of the high school curriculum, and community colleges gained some traction from this period on by incorporating vocational education into the curriculum.[6] Early in their development, community colleges offered programs in trades such as welding, air conditioning repair, and truck driving, which predated advanced technologies in computing in the 1980s and 1990s. During the past decade, it is heath occupations which have seen the greatest growth in enrolments.[7]

While the academic community is divided on the benefits of CTE, policy makers tend to be much more supportive. The Federal government provides funding for CTE programs through the Carl D. Perkins Vocational and Technical Education Act. The 2006 reauthorization of the Act emphasized high school to college transition, academic achievement of CTE students, and state and local accountability. President Obama has endorsed the role of community colleges in spurring economic growth through policy addresses notably at Macomb Community College in Michigan and Northern Virginia Community College. In his 2012 State of the Union Address, Obama called for community colleges to serve as career centers to encourage and stimulate economic recovery: "Now you need to give more community colleges the resources they need to become community career centers—places that teach people skills that businesses are looking for right now, from data management to high-tech manufacturing." All of this is a way of saying that policy makers may envision a more prominent vocational role for community colleges than their own faculty and administrators.

SOME COLLEGE IS BETTER THAN NO COLLEGE

From the perspective of students, a primary purpose of higher education is to prepare them for work. For many community college students, the hope is that postsecondary education will lead to a bachelor's degree and beyond, but financial realities are ever present. In ethnographic research conducted in community college classrooms, Cox found equating higher levels of education with an improved job outlook was a primary source of motivation for students. Students consistently "explained their participation in higher education as a means to earn a decent living and reach financial stability."[8] Community college students tend to describe their aspirations in occupational terms, and engage in personalized cost benefit analysis which crystallizes decision making around the expectation that college education will have a "pay off."[9] Grubb describes this approach to education as "vocationalist" in that even students who are not enrolled in vocational programs have vocational goals.[10]

Students are correct in thinking that higher education pays off. Based on 2007–2009 American Community Survey data, individuals holding bachelor's degrees earn on average 84 percent more over a lifetime than high school graduates. This is approximately nine percent higher than in 2002, suggesting that the premium on earning a bachelor's degree is growing.[11] Even "some college" without a degree leads to an annual earnings increase of $38,700.[12] Carnevale et al. conclude that "the data are clear: a college degree is key to economic opportunity, conferring substantially higher earnings on those with credentials than those without."[13]

Economists concur that the sacrifices involved in pursuing a degree or certificate at a community college pay off. Even completing one year of community college coursework is associated with earning gains.[14] There are numerous studies of the financial returns to postsecondary education, and even some dealing with aggregate social benefits at the local or state level.[15] The majority of studies use national longitudinal datasets, for example the Beginning Postsecondary Study (BPS) and the NELS:88. Although these surveys were initiated in the 1980s and 1990s, one of the challenges of understanding economic returns of education is that fact that it may take years for students to realize discernible outcomes. National surveys are comprehensive in terms of providing data on occupations and salaries. By comparison, state datasets typically do not follow students for a long enough period of time and lose data on students who work across state lines.

Individuals earning Associate degrees have higher earnings than those who did not complete high school.[16] Marcotte et al. estimated that men holding Associate degrees earned 14.7 percent more than their peers with a high school education and women earned 47.6 percent more annually.[17] Because of the high incidence of students leaving community college without graduating, researchers have taken a special interest in measuring financial returns to coursework with and without a degree or certificate. [18] The hypothesis in these studies is that students holding an Associate degree or certificate earn more than those who only took the coursework, since the degree serves as a "signal" of skill development to employers. Results of these studies are inconclusive although they generally tend to indicate that the degree itself seems to hold value over and above completing the coursework. Differences are linked to specific majors. However, coursework for students completing only half a full-time equivalent year or less had almost no earnings effect. [19]

A factor that complicates the employment outcomes of community college students is the fact that many are already working while they are in college. Estimates suggest that 45.4 percent of full-time students and 71.8 percent of part-time students work while attending community college. [20] The 2011 CCSSE survey findings are consistent with these estimates, indicating that among the nearly 435,000 community college students surveyed, nearly a third are working more than thirty hours a week while attending college, and nearly half are working more than twenty hours a week.

The type of work that community college students obtain while attending college is not likely to be highly paid, since most do not hold a college degree. Carnevale, Rose, and Chea found that a person holding an Associate degree earns an average of $20.77 per hour, compared with $15.67 per hour for an individual holding only a high school diploma. [21] The kinds of jobs students without college degrees are most likely to obtain include sales, driving, retail, secretarial work, nursing and health aides, janitorial, or labor

Table 4.2 16-24 Year Old College Students Who Were Employed, October 2009 (NCES 2011, Table A-45-1)

		Hours worked per week*		
	Percent employed†	**Less than 20 hours**	**20–34 hours**	**35 or more hours**
Full-time	45.4	16.0	20.5	7.8
Part-time	71.8	10.3	30.6	29.4

* Excludes those who were employed but not at work during the survey week; therefore, detail may not sum to total percentage employed. Hours worked per week refers to the number of hours the respondent worked at all jobs during the survey week.
† Includes those who were employed but not at work during the survey week.
SOURCE: U.S. Department of Commerce, Census Bureau, Current Population Survey (CPS), October Supplement, selected years, 1970–2009.

work.[22] What the data and charts do not easily capture is that many of these jobs require working night shifts and weekends.

Research generally shows a positive impact on educational outcomes for students working only a few hours a week, but a negative impact for those working more.[23] It is not only the stress of time spent at work, but the underlying reasons for having to work so many hours that lead to long-term problems for students. For instance, students must work during college because they are paying their own way, are financially independent, and have family obligations.

The stress that accompanies low income and limited resources presents a significant barrier to college completion for many community college students. Survey results link the problem of having to work to pay for college and living expenses with decisions to drop out or delay degree completion by stopping out or attending part-time. Public Agenda recently surveyed 600 young adults aged twenty-two to thirty, who had at least some higher education, about their decisions regarding degree completion or leaving college without a degree.[24] Researchers found that having to work was the top reason young adults give for leaving college. Overall, 71 percent cited needing to work to make money as the reason to leave school, and 54 percent of these respondents described it as a "major reason."[25] The second most frequent explanation was that they could not afford tuition and fees (52 percent). Most telling, 60 percent of the students leaving college without a degree said they had to pay for college themselves, while conversely 60 percent of those completing degrees said they had help covering tuition from parents and relatives.[26] Difficulties relating to teaching and learning or a lack of motivation were cited least often.

Research on the academic success of community college CTE students is limited. Bailey at al. used two national datasets to analyze graduation and transfer rates of community college students.[27] Their analysis contrasted the outcomes of occupational students starting at four-year colleges with those starting at community colleges. The results showed that students starting in baccalaureate degree programs achieved the most favorable outcomes, followed by those in certificate programs. Students starting in occupation Associate degree programs had noncompletion rates that were 10 to 20 percent higher than students in other program categories.

MEASURING OCCUPATIONAL OUTCOMES

As with other areas of community college research, large-scale national datasets provide much of what we know about career and technical education. These datasets include the Beginning Postsecondary Survey (BPS), NELS:88; and the National Postsecondary Student Aid Study (NPSAS). Data providing information to colleges on the efficacy of their CTE programs are notoriously difficult to obtain. As a result, institutions rely heavily on feedback from program advisory committees and graduate surveys to gather this information. Advisory committees provide very little in the way of comprehensive information. The role that they play varies, as does meeting frequency and size.[28] Graduate surveys also provide limited data because of difficulty in obtaining high response rates from graduates. Furthermore, many community college students enter the workforce prior to graduation thereby rendering surveys of graduates ineffective in providing a comprehensive picture of student outcomes.

One method for efficiently gathering labor statistics is available through Economic Modeling Specialists, Inc. (EMSI). EMSI draws on more than ninety data sources, including Bureau of Labor Statistics and state and private sources, to provide current information about job growth and decline in specified regions and counties. The data are delivered online in a customizable reporting format specific to academic programs on community college campuses. It can be used by researchers and college administrators alike for planning purposes. It is also a useful tool for career counselors.

Career Coach is a tool provided by EMSI that turns data into information. This is an online service that enables students to learn about job earnings, employment trends, and the education and training needed for specific job types. Like other EMSI products, Career Coach is customized to draw on data for the counties and region served by a college. Montgomery County Community College in Pennsylvania and Miami Dade College in Florida are institutions currently using Career Coach.

In 2011, the Obama administration put into place new regulations to inform students about the earnings of CTE graduates. The purpose of the new regulations is to protect students against programs that do not lead to "gainful employment." Colleges are now required to report graduation and employment statistics for CTE programs that qualify under this legislation. While the new regulations were aimed primarily at the for-profit sector, they are requiring community colleges to become more sophisticated in data collection related to completion and employment.

EMBRACING THE ECONOMIC LIVES OF COMMUNITY COLLEGE STUDENTS

The impact of the "vocationalist" perspective held by community college students on retention is not well understood. While students will readily identify transfer and long-term academic goals, their ultimate focus is on employment. Obtaining employable skills provides a strong motivation for students, many of whom are struggling financially and wish for a better quality of life. Unfortunately, this simple fact is overlooked by many community colleges. Rather than organizing curricula around employment as a motivating factor, community colleges remain focused on the liberal arts.[29] As a consequence, CTE programs are marginalized at community colleges, taught by a workforce of adjunct faculty, and located in distant hallways and buildings.

For the large number of students who cannot identify a specific major field or career goal, rather than facilitating choice by helping them sort through information, community colleges enroll them in generic majors such as "general studies" or "liberal arts." By failing to embrace the economic lives of students and leverage their desire to get jobs, community colleges are missing a major opportunity to engage students and motivate them to degree completion. Innovation is underway in this area and CTE educators and organizations concerned with social welfare are involved in strengthening career education and finding ways to broaden its reach. Much remains to be done, however, and harnessing the full benefit of CTE remains a formidable challenge to community colleges.

The Pedagogical Secrets of CTE

Despite the importance of employment to students, career education struggles with status problems. Occupational programs are often not well understood by faculty in part because of the specificity of their curricula. However, there is also a degree of physical isolation from other programs that comes with the turf in CTE programs. Career programs require specialized classrooms, such as laboratories, kitchens, simulated hospital settings, or early childhood centers. In general, they have high overhead costs, take up more space than liberal arts programs, and have specialized equipment that needs to be protected. As a result, many of the interesting and cutting edge educational practices present in career programs remain hidden from students' view, even as they are showcased for visitors.

Practices common to CTE teaching and learning promote student success as discussed earlier. A number of programs—nursing, early childhood education, and engineering, to name a few—have accountability practices driven by program accreditation and licensure exams. For example, the National Association for the Education of Young Children (NAEYC) provides accredited programs with standards and has established student learning outcomes and rubrics with which to measure progress toward meeting standards. The hands-on nature of learning in occupational programs mandates that curricula include experiential learning, cooperative learning, and demonstrable student outcomes. And the organization of the class schedules and use of labs and faculty result in students having the opportunity to bond with others in their cohort as they take multiple classes together. Based on a large-scale study involving extensive classroom observations, Grubb and Associates found that "for many fields, occupational teaching turns out to be rich and complex, more so than teaching in academic subjects. In most occupations there are many competencies to master, including manual and visual abilities, problem solving and interpersonal skills as well as conventional linguistic and mathematical abilities.[30] The literacy practices are varied and sophisticated, though quite different from academic classes."[31]

CTE educators are also innovating by "stacking" courses in their programs. The purpose of a stackable curriculum is to give students opportunities to reach short-term completion points on their way to a degree or certificate. The rationale underlying this approach is that students will achieve greater success in the workforce if they have completed a sequence of courses. The short-term completion points are stacked up to make it easier for students to move fluidly between college and work. In this way, a student may finish a three-course sequence at one juncture and then add a certificate later, eventually returning at a later date to work toward a degree. For example, Maricopa College in Arizona offers a Certificate of General Education, Certificate of Completion, and Certificate of Competency as a way of chunking up its CTE programs.

The Advanced Technological Education (ATE) Program

The ATE program is funded through the National Science Foundation and was initiated by Congress in 1992 under the Scientific and Advanced Technology Act (SATA). The program stipulates that community colleges partner with four-year colleges and universities, secondary schools, business, industry, and government, to respond to employer needs for well-prepared technicians in the fields of science, technology, engineering, and mathematics (STEM). The overarching goal is to produce more qualified science and engineering technicians to meet workforce demands. Over the past decade, hundreds of community colleges have been funded to develop and expand programs that will prepare technicians in emerging technologies.

There are currently thirty-eight ATE Centers forming the backbone of the program. In fiscal year 2012, newly funded centers received up to $1.4 million over four years to create partnerships and networks around program and curriculum development in STEM fields. Examples of ATE include:

> Bio-Link: Started at the City College of San Francisco in 1998 with the goal of developing a biotechnology curriculum in partnership with the University of San Francisco and biotech businesses. The Center develops curricula and provides support to biotech programs at community colleges across the country. It also sponsors and coordinates a summer conference for biotech faculty.

SCATE: The South Carolina Advanced Technological Education Center-Center of Excellence has been in existence since 1996. It has developed an integrated, problem-based curriculum, collaborative teaching strategies and extensive active learning techniques to strengthen teaching and learning in engineering technology.

BATEC: The Boston Area Advanced Technological Education Connections is focused on improving technician education in information technology. The Center partners with high schools, provides professional development to hundreds of high school and community college instructors annually, and has established a "Bridge to Community College" program for adult learners, which combines credit-bearing technology courses with English and mathematics tutoring and delivers workshops on college admissions, financial aid, course registration, and advising.

The ATE program has infused millions of dollars ($64 million in fiscal year 2012 alone) into the development and improvement of CTE education at community colleges. The theory underlying this reform focuses on networks of practitioners. Recipients of ATE funding meet annually at a national conference where they exchange ideas and learn about campus-based projects. The ATE program has made it possible for community colleges to obtain the financial resources to develop sophisticated programs in cutting edge occupations.

Center for Working Families

Another approach to strengthening connections with the workforce involves embracing students as workers. The Center for Working Families (CWF) model, developed and funded by the Annie E. Casey Foundation, is one such initiative.[32] The focus of the Centers is on helping low income families reach financial security and improve their income and economic outlook. This initiative involves bundling services so that they are convenient and comprehensive for families. Services incorporated into the program include improving financial literacy, providing financial support, employment and career advancement services, income enhancement and work supports, and financial and wealth-building services. One of a few centers located on a community college campus is at Central New Mexico Community College (CNMC).

At CNMC, the Center for Working Families is part of the School of Adult and General Education, which provides developmental education. Students are referred to CWF by faculty and through outreach. They are able to meet with an "achievement coach" who assists students in developing a plan to overcome obstacles such as expenses for child care, books and transportation that might interfere with their ability to stay in school. Students also participate in financial literacy workshops, where they learn how to prepare a household budget, prepare tax forms, and engage in public benefit screening.

An option for benefit screening includes Single Stop. Single Stop U.S.A. was established in 2007 and grew out of Single Stop NY, which was funded by the Robin Hood Foundation. This initiative puts people in contact with the public benefits to which they are entitled. Like the Center for Working Families, Single Stop bundles services to make it easier and quicker for students to get the financial help they need to stay in school. Services provided include free tax preparation, full benefits access, comprehensive legal services, and financial counseling. A major component of the service involves screening participants to determine which public benefits they could be receiving and streamlining paperwork to help them acquire the benefits. Preliminary results are promising: students receiving bundled services succeed economically at higher rates than those who receive only one service.[33]

LEARNING FROM WORKFORCE DEVELOPMENT

Community colleges would do well to make workforce preparation central to their vision of educational delivery. By this, I do not imply a return to "terminal" degrees and purely vocational education. Instead, it is obvious from the innovations already underway that linking community college education to jobs and the workforce provides greatly needed focus and relevance. There are many contact points at which CTE could be infused into the curriculum in ways that will capture students' interest and connect with their "vocationalist" motivation for attending college.

As students move through the application and orientation process, it is possible to administer career inventories and offer the option to complete online career exploration activities. College websites can provide students with concrete information about school to career pathways. Some colleges offer learning communities to students in their first year of college that link remedial courses with occupational courses. Bronx Community College recently undertook a reform of its student success course by replacing it with a content-driven course. Students took courses in areas such as forensics and early childhood that they might never have experienced were they not integrated into the student success course. Programs such as I-BEST are also demonstrating the benefits of contextualizing developmental education by linking it with occupational skill development.

In the intermediary stages of college life, programs could be offered that help students develop networks with the community and local employers that could engage and motivate them to completion. Hirschy et al. define this dimension as "career integration"—the idea that "meaningful career-related experiences may occur on- and off-campus and because the boundaries between school and work are permeable."[34] Rather than struggling with the fact that students need to work, and in many cases work long hours, greater success for students may be achieved by blurring the boundaries between college and the community. Service learning is one way to integrate experiential learning into the curriculum so that students can complete their coursework, while at the same time applying knowledge gained in class to helping others in the community. The Center for Working Families provides a different kind of model, where students are taught strategies for balancing school and work and strengthening their financial circumstances.

As students reach graduation, they must be prepared for transitioning into the workforce or to a four-year college. At this stage, internships, co-ops and clinical experiences could help students strengthen and apply occupational skills. Colleges can also make it possible for students to demonstrate their skills to employers through e-portfolios. An e-portfolio is made up of samples of a student's work, which can include images and videos as well as documents. E-portfolios are now commonly used by instructors to measure student learning outcomes in programs.

The focus on career preparation can be continued even after graduation. Today's community college graduates and transfers become tomorrow's employers. Community colleges have not emphasized alumni relations in part because of difficulty in tracking alumni in an institution where students enter and exit rapidly. Furthermore, community colleges do not possess sufficient resources for managing large alumni databases or organizing events. Nevertheless, strengthening relations with business and industry as well as leveraging inexpensive mechanisms such as social media to keep students "in the loop" can put colleges in touch with their alumni. Alumni connections can provide colleges with internships, service learning opportunities, and mentoring for current students, not to mention improving communication and goodwill with local employers.

NOTES

1. Russell Rumberger, "Education and the Reproduction of Economic Inequality in the United States: An Empirical Investigation," *Economics of Education Review* 29(2009), 251–2.

2. Ibid., 252.

3. Regina Diel-Amen and James E. Rosenbaum, "The Social Prerequisites of Success: Can College Structure Reduce the Need for Social Know-How? " *Annals of the American Academy of Political and Social Science* 586, no. 1 (2003).

4. NCES, "Condition of Education," (Washginton, DC: National Center for Education Statistics, 2011).

5. Amy S. Hirschy, Christine D Bremer, and Marisa Castellano, "Career and Technical Education (Cte) Student Success in Community Colleges: A Conceptual Model," *Community College Review* 39, no. 3 (2011), 298.

6. Steven Brint and Jerome Karabel, *The Diverted Dream: Community Colleges and the Promise of Educational Opportunity in America, 1900 - 1985* (New York: Oxford University Press, 1989); Kevin J. Dougherty, *The Contradictory College: The Conflicting Origins, Im-*

pacts, and Futures of the Community Colleges (Albany, NY: State University of New York Press, 1994).

7. Karen Levesque et al., "Career and Technical Education in the United States: 1990 to 2005," (Washington, DC: National Center for Education Statistics, 2008).

8. Rebecca D. Cox, *The College Fear Factor: How Students and Professors Misunderstand One Another* (Cambridge, MA: Harvard University Press, 2009), 42.

9. Ibid.; James R. Valadez, "Preparing for Work in a Post-Industrial World: Resistance and Compliance to the Ideological Messages of a Community College," in *Community Colleges as Cultural Texts: Qualitative Explorations of Organizational and Student Culture*, ed. Kathleen M. Shaw, James R. Valadez, and Robert A. Rhoads (Albany: SUNY Press, 1999).

10. Norton Grubb, "Learning and Earning in the Middle: The Economic Benefits of Sub-Baccalaureate Education," (New York: Community College Research Center, Teachers College, Columbia University, 1999); Norton Grubb, "Learning and Earning in the Middle, Part I: National Studies of Pre-Baccalaureate Education," *Economics of Education Review* 21(2002); W. Norton Grubb, *Honored but Invisible: An inside Look at Teaching in Community Colleges* (New York: Routledge, 1999).

11. Anthony P. Carnevale, Stephen J. Rose, and Ban Cheah, "The College Payoff: Education, Occupations, Lifetime Earnings," (Washington DC. Georgetown University Center on Education and the Workforce, 2011).

12. Ibid., 4.

13. Ibid., 1.

14. Thomas J. Kane and Celia E. Rouse, "The Community College: Educating Students at the Margin between College and Work," *The Journal of Economic Perspectives* 13, no. 1 (1999).

15. Clive Belfield and Thomas Bailey, "The Benefits of Attending Community College: A Review of the Evidence," *Community college Review* 39, no. 1 (2011).

16. Grubb, "Learning and Earning in the Middle: The Economic Benefits of Sub-Baccalaureate Education."; Kane and Rouse, "The Community College: Educating Students at the Margin between College and Work."; D. E. Marcotte et al., "The Returns of a Community College Education: Evidence from the National Education Longitudinal Survey," *Educational Evaluation and Policy Analysis* 27, no. 2 (2005).

17. D. E. Marcotte et al., "The Returns of a Community College Education: Evidence from the National Education Longitudinal Survey," 166.

18. Grubb, "Learning and Earning in the Middle, Part I: National Studies of Pre-Baccalaureate Education."; Marcotte et al., "The Returns of a Community College Education: Evidence from the National Education Longitudinal Survey."

19. Grubb, "Learning and Earning in the Middle, Part I: National Studies of Pre-Baccalaureate Education."

20. NCES, "Condition of Education."; ibid., Table A-45-1.

21. Carnevale, Rose, and Cheah, "The College Payoff: Education, Occupations, Lifetime Earnings," 3.

22. Ibid., 14.

23. Alexander Astin, *What Matters in College? Four Critical Years Revisited.* (San Francisco: Jossey-Bass, 1993).

24. Jean Johnson and Jon Rochkind, "One Degree of Separation: How Young Americans Who Don't Finish College See Their Chances of Success," (New York: Public Agenda).

25. Ibid., 7.

26. Ibid., 9.

27. Thomas Bailey et al., "Educational Outcomes of Postsecondary Occupational Students," (New York: Community College Research Center, Teachers College, Columbia University, 2004).

28. Grubb, "Learning and Earning in the Middle: The Economic Benefits of Sub-Baccalaureate Education."

29. Ibid.

30. Grubb, *Honored but Invisible: An inside Look at Teaching in Community Colleges.*

31. Ibid., 99.

32. Center for Working Families
33. Center for Working Families, 12.
34. Hirschy, Bremer, and Castellano, "Career and Technical Education (CTE) Student Success in Community Colleges: A Conceptual Model," 312,

Chapter Five

A Complex Equation: Transfer and Student Success

Many, if not most, high school students see themselves earning at least a bachelor's degree at some point in the future. Increasingly, adult learners are returning to school with the same goal. In my conversations with students, I often find younger students are not sure of what career they will pursue, but know that they want to be college graduates. Adult students, on the other hand, are more pragmatic and perceive the degree as a *need* rather than a *want*. As we have seen in previous chapters, the majority of those starting at community colleges will not reach this milestone on the first attempt. Some will find that academic weaknesses get in the way. Others will become adrift in the institution without a full understanding of how to connect with the people who are there to help. Yet others will discover that they cannot afford college or handle the stress of juggling school and work. In all too many cases, these problems are present at the same time.

For many students, transfer is a long-term and ill-defined goal. To achieve it may require years of coursework and personal sacrifice. Once success is near, reality sets in and students are bombarded with multiple challenges as they prepare for transition to a new institution. They wonder how they will pay for tuition, whether they will be able to attend college locally or will have move, and whether they have the ability to succeed in a four-year institution. All are important questions, and transfer students must rely on admissions counselors at their transfer institution to get accurate answers. If a student is considering multiple institutions this could entail numerous contacts and significant time and effort.

The issue of transfer is, and always has been, a lightning rod in the literature on community colleges. Levin et al.[1] argue that too much focus on transfer not only puts community colleges in a negative light, but distracts from important missions of the colleges. Some argue that because the chances of earning a bachelor's degree are slim for many students, community colleges should scale back the focus on transfer and emphasizes short-term goals in occupational and career programs. Indeed, many occupational programs have both transfer and terminal options, because career advancement in most fields ultimately calls for earning a bachelor's degree. And, as described in the previous chapter, earnings from an Associate degree are substantially lower than those linked with earning a bachelor's degree.

Our knowledge about processes and outcomes of community college transfer are shaped by important limitations in the available data. After all, multiple institutions must be involved in data collection in order to track students as they move through the system. Understanding what we know about transfer first requires developing an understanding about the information on which research is based.

DATA SOURCES ON TRANSFER

National surveys have provided rich data on transfer. National Educational Longitudinal Survey (NELS) data have been used in several recent studies of transfer because they provide transcript data specific to institutions. Transcript data are composed of information specific to courses taken and grades earned. This is considered to be the most reliable source of information when analyzing student transfer because self-reported information is not reliable.[2] However, interpreting transcript data can be a major challenge, as categorizing courses using course numbering systems, the names of courses, and subject or department codes is inconsistent at best.

National data sets such as NELS:88 have routinely been used to construct basic scientific knowledge about transfer student behavior and outcomes but are a less useful analysis of articulation and short-term outcomes. This is because the number of community college students in the sample who successfully transferred is not large. For example, Meguizo at al. base their analysis on 3,160 students in the NELS:88 sample, of whom 640 started at a two-year college.[3]

More powerful data on transfer are available at the state and institutional levels, particularly in systems that have centralized data systems. The data source most widely used by institutional and state researchers to study transfer behavior is the National Student Clearinghouse (NSC). NSC is a nonprofit organization established in 1993 as a repository for student information. The organization's core purpose is to make the process of exchanging information about student enrollment and degree and certificate completion more efficient and timely for the purposes of granting financial aid. According to NSC, approximately 93 percent of all postsecondary students are in their database, which represents the student population at more than 3,300 colleges and universities.[4] Colleges routinely upload data on registered students and graduates which enables the database to verify the progress of students at participating colleges.

For the purpose of studying transfer, NSC provides colleges and universities with a StudentTracker service. Through this service, colleges and universities can query the database for information specific to their students. The data are returned with information similar to table 5.1 (see next section), in which a data outlay is provided for each student for each semester that he or she is enrolled after a stated semester. Researchers are able to observe transfer and multi-institutional attendance and trace degrees or certificates granted to students, the semester in which they graduated, and their majors. Needless to say, this is a rich source of data, because it captures transfer to public and private institutions, as well as lateral transfer to like-type institutions. The only downside is that the data are not complete as a few colleges in the country do not participate.

THE HORIZONTAL AND VERTICAL ASPECTS OF TRANSFER

Transcript analysis and student tracking have enabled researchers to better understand just how transient college students are. Multi-institutional attendance patterns (i.e., swirling) first became apparent to researchers in the late 1980s and were documented in the literature during the 1990s through analysis of national datasets.[5] What researchers learned is that by the 1990s, less than half of the nation's undergraduates attended only one institution.[6] In fact, as many as 20 percent of the students studied attended more than two institutions over the course of their college careers. Research on transfer behaviors revealed that this pattern was as prevalent among four-year college and university students as among community college students. Furthermore, students do not necessarily follow a progression of starting at a community college and transferring to a four-year institution, rather they flow in all directions between and within sectors. We also know from college-level data that students attend multiple institutions during the same semester; for example, taking a math class at a community college and a business course at a four-year university.

Swirling patterns wreak havoc on analyses of student success. Even researchers devoting painstaking attention to data analysis have trouble categorizing transfers, ultimately leading to a concern of how to define a transfer student.[7] Sylvia, Song and Waters provided the following definitional possibilities that have been used by researchers studying transfer:[8]

- Transferred to a public four-year college

• Enrolled at any four-year college after leaving a two-year college
• Took one or more classes at any four-year college within four years
• Have two-year college credit on their transcripts

In other words, there are so many permutations of the definition of transfer and associated behavior that there is an absence of consensus about the success of transfer students.

Table 5.1 illustrates the complexity of analyzing transfer outcomes using NSC data. The student in this example enrolled in a two-year college and attended continuously until spring of 2008, when she transferred to a public university. If the story ended there (or with a bachelor's degree a few years later) everything would be straightforward. However, after a year, the student took a semester off and then returned to the community college for a year, but this time at a different community college. Eventually, the student showed up at a fourth institution, this time another public four-year institution. Within a six-year time period, this student's enrollment behavior exhibited twists and turns that are common to community college students:

• Transfer without Associate degree completion
• Stop-out
• Reverse transfer
• Multi-institution attendance

The translation of this student's behavior into a measurable outcome is entirely dependent upon the time frame being analyzed. From the perspective of the student's first institution of enrollment, Metro Community College, this student would not count as a success because she failed to graduate within a reasonable period of time. She would count for Metro Community College as a transfer without degree, because by fall 2008 the student was enrolled at a four-year college. From the perspective of Valley Community College, this student is a "transfer student" because she transferred into the institution. However, does this really represent 'transfer? Probably not, because there is no indication in this student's trajectory of intention to complete an Associate degree. Using a six-year time to degree measure, the student would be considered a successful transfer student for Metro Community College. But is this really success? We should also not rule out the Associate degree in the long run, because our sample student is banking credits at a number of institutions. In the end, she may face a practical decision about where to complete a degree based on factors such as geographic proximity, the institution that will accept the most credits, and the one that makes the process of transferring credits easiest.

There are many challenges inherent in analyzing transfer and swirling patterns. In research on transfer patterns, Adelman coded the "referent" insti-

Table 5.1 Transfer Student Raw Data Six-years from Fall 2005 to Spring 2011

College	Level	Sector	Semester
METRO COMMUNITY COLLEGE	2	Public	Fall 2005
METRO COMMUNITY COLLEGE	2	Public	Spring 2006
METRO COMMUNITY COLLEGE	2	Public	Fall 2006
METRO COMMUNITY COLLEGE	2	Public	Spring 2007
METRO COMMUNITY COLLEGE	2	Public	Fall 2007
WESTERN STATE UNIVERSITY	4	Public	Spring 2008
WESTERN STATE UNIVERSITY	4	Public	Fall 2008
Not enrolled	--	--	Spring 2009
VALLEY COMMUNITY COLLEGE	2	Public	Fall 2009
VALLEY COMMUNITY COLLEGE	2	Public	Spring 2010
SOUTHERN STATE UNIVERSITY	4	Public	Fall 2010
Not enrolled	--	--	Spring 2011

tution—the institution that seemed to be "home" for the student in terms of attendance—and found that among all postsecondary students, the greatest incidence of multi-institutional attendance was among community colleges (22 percent), followed by community college to four-year institution (10 percent) and alternating or simultaneous community college and four-year institution (5 percent) and four-year institution to community college or "reverse transfer" (4 percent).[9] If we look solely at community college students, Adelman estimated a transfer rate of about 26 percent. This transfer rate is appreciably higher than national estimates using student right to know data which evidenced a three-year transfer rate of 17.6 percent for first-time, full-time degree-seeking students in the 2006 cohort.[10]

Reverse transfer occurs when students transfer from four-year colleges and universities to two-year colleges. In a recent analysis of reverse transfer, Kalogrides and Grodsky found that this phenomenon more than tripled between 1972 and 1996, and that reverse transfer students make up roughly 11 percent of those who leave four-year colleges and universities.[11] Reverse transfer is a phenomenon contributing to the educational diversity of community colleges, and it follows at least three different enrollment patterns. One pattern involves bachelor's degree students who revise their educational and career plans by transferring to two-year institutions. But this definition can also apply to students who are moving back and forth between the two types of institutions with the bachelor's degree as a goal, as well as students who have already completed a bachelor's degree.[12]

An NCES study using 1989–1990 Beginning Postsecondary Survey data, further demonstrates the complexity of multi-institutional attendance and the extent to which research results can be influenced by swirling. In this study, the researchers used nine definitions of "transfer student" to analyze the degree to which changes in the denominator result in different transfer rates. Among all students, 25.4 percent eventually transferred to a four-year institution. Among students declaring transfer as their goal, the number increased to 35.7 percent. As the definition narrowed, the transfer rate continued to rise. Among students pursuing an academic major and taking courses toward a bachelor's degree, the transfer rate approximated 52.3 percent. [13]

OPTIMIZING FOR SUCCESS

There are a number of operational considerations associated with student success in an environment where swirling is commonplace. If we approach success from the standpoint of vertical movement through the institution, the baseline would be learners entering as first-time students whose primary goal is transfer. In order to accommodate these students, community colleges have developed a wide range of transfer programs, the most fundamental of which are described as "liberal arts" or "general studies." These programs are geared toward offering students a general education curriculum, which includes mathematics, English, social sciences, sciences, arts, and humanities; the courses they would be taking in the first two years at a four-year college.

In addition, community colleges offer occupationally oriented transfer programs in fields such as business, criminal justice, early childhood, hospitality, and others. In many cases, the difference between terminal and transfer degrees in these fields can be the option to take an advanced applied mathematics or writing course as opposed to the college level courses required to complete the program. The difference tends to be so subtle that even experienced students must discuss their course choices with an advisor in order to understand the nuances of course selection decisions.

For many students, these discussions occur when graduation is in sight, rather than earlier in their college career. As a result, students often find that additional course work is necessary in order to transfer. Top-notch advising is critical and must occur at an early point in students' community college experience to ensure the choice of courses will earn the expected credit at the next level. The ratio of students to counselors at community colleges is extraordinarily high. At many colleges, instructors make a significant contribution to student advising, but many admit that they find it difficult to remain current with transfer intricacies and changes. When looking at optimizing student success it is critical to consider not only the advising that students receive, but also what they do not. [14] Three decades ago, sociologist Burton Clark described the "blurred" distinction between transfer and terminal degrees, where colleges were "reducing as much as possible the labeling of courses and curricula as transfer and non-transfer, and hence the parallel self-labeling of students in one track or the other." [15] While the message given to community college students is one of openness and access, the reality is that successful transfer hinges on limiting options and specifying very early on, with the help of an experienced advisor, the curriculum that will move students toward their academic goals.

THE ART OF ARTICULATION

Underlying course selection for transfer students is articulation. Articulation refers to the negotiated equivalency of courses taken in different institutions. The question of whether a community college English 101 course will be accepted as equivalent to English 101 at another institution is one that can be shaped by external forces. Specifically, the presence of state or system level policies that provide students with leverage is important to understanding the student transfer experience. If vertical alignment is lacking in processes through which states drive articulation negotiations between four-year institutions and community colleges, the responsibility for establishing articulation agreements drops to the departmental level. This means that whether a university will accept a course as basic as English 101 toward fulfilling degree requirements relies on an agreement between community college faculty and their university counterparts. The number of credits or the choice of textbook can ultimately determine whether a student will receive credit for a community college course.

The role of elective credits in community college transfer receives little attention in the literature but can be critical to community college students wishing to transfer. Universities may offer community college students credit for coursework which counts toward elective credits but not toward degree requirements in the major. To some extent, elective credit is a compromise resulting from conflict of interest. In courses that are specialized—as opposed to those deemed to be general education—faculty at both levels must achieve enrollment quotas if their courses are to make. This fosters competitive tension. Four-year institutions are organized around the assumption that general education courses will be taken during the first two years, and courses in the career major in the junior and senior years. However, community colleges combine general education and courses in the major into a two-year degree.

When students take courses in a major during the first two years, it creates a dilemma upon transfer. At both levels, faculty control the process for determining educational learning priorities for their majors, and the curriculum builds knowledge through sequential courses. Community college transfers may be underprepared in their major if the learning outcomes of community college courses are not carefully aligned with the four-year curriculum. As a result, students may not be granted credit for courses taken at the community college. Learners who have been led to believe that they are working toward a baccalaureate degree by starting at a community college can become victims of weak articulation between institutions. This is a systemic problem that impacts the success of transfer students and that requires vertical alignment.

OUTCOMES OF TRANSFER STUDENTS

The success of transfer as a community college function is hotly debated. While transfer students generally perform well at four-year colleges, the small proportion of students who actually succeed in transfer tempers success of the overall endeavor. The reason for the debate surrounding transfer therefore is that we do not know whether students who attend community college would have been able to attend college at all if it were not for the transfer option. Since students choose community colleges because they are lower cost and close to home, one could deduce that college simply would not be an option for many students if it weren't for community colleges. Indeed, the evidence suggests that multi-institutional attendance is more common among low SES students than high SES students.[16] Goldrick-Rab found that not only are low SES students four times more likely than others to transfer between institutions, they are also four times more likely to take time off during these transitions.[17]

Celia Rouse, in an influential paper about community college transfer, asked whether community colleges democratize higher education by making college accessible to a broader cross-section of students, or whether the availability of community colleges draws students away from starting at a four-year colleges, which have higher graduation rates.[18] Rouse concluded that even though community college students completed fewer years of college, this did not seem to lower the overall baccalaureate attainment rate.

Propensity scoring (described in chapter 2) provides researchers with a statistical method for controlling for self-selection bias in transfer. This is a particularly useful technique with regard to community college students, since students who choose to attend community colleges are different in both observable and unobservable ways from students choosing to attend four-year colleges. Propensity scoring simulates an experimental design so that students who have the option of attending a two-year or four-year college can be compared, and a choice to attend a two-year college becomes a "treatment." Using this technique, we can determine whether attending a community college as opposed to starting at a four-year institution has an effect on the outcomes of similar students. Results show no statistical difference between transfer students and native four-year students with respect to the likelihood of graduation or the number of credits earned.[19] The research tells us that low transfer rates are the problem, rather than lower success rates of transfer students once they reach baccalaureate institutions.

CRITICAL ROLE OF THE STATES

Policy makers have a critical role to play in improving the success of community college transfer. In order for transfer to serve as an efficient way for students to earn a bachelor's degree, cooperation across numerous institutions is required. From the perspective of four-year colleges and universities, students may be transferring from different community colleges throughout the state. They will have been exposed to a wide range of curricula delivered by instructors whose backgrounds and credentials are likely to be much more varied than those of university faculty by virtue of the hiring, promotion, and tenure processes employed by community colleges. It is understandable that universities are wary of variation in the academic preparation of community college students. Nonetheless, a state supported system of articulation between community colleges and four-year colleges and universities is a viable route to degree completion. States have a responsibility to make these systems work.

Among states with large community college systems, a consensus is emerging that a general education core curriculum articulated with public universities is feasible. A number of states have taken steps to create these systems, including Texas and Washington, which have initiated work on curriculum agreements in career majors such as business, education, and nursing. A recent report by the Center for the Study of Community Colleges at UCLA outlines the characteristics of effective state articulation policies:[20]

Essential elements:

1. A common general education package
2. Common lower-division pre-major and early-major pathways
3. A focus on credit applicability, in other words, transfer credits must count toward degree requirements and not just electives
4. Junior status upon transfer

Helpful elements:

1. Guaranteed and/or priority university admission to students meeting specific criteria, such as completing an Associate degree
2. Associate and/or bachelor's degree credit limits, which make it difficult for programs to add credits as a way of accommodating the core curriculum

3. An acceptance policy for upper-division courses, which states that specific courses will be accepted as equivalent to those in the university degree program

The UCLA report is detailed in its review of the elements that contribute to the development of statewide plans in states such as Arizona, Ohio, New Jersey, and Washington. Ensuring that policies are broadly adopted requires cooperation and coordination at every level of the system, from legislators to instructors.

STATE TRANSFER POLICY AT WORK

The State of Washington has been working to increase the scope and success of transfer over the past several years. Some success has been achieved through (a) establishing statewide articulation; (b) the availability of three degree pathways leading to transfer; and (c) a dual enrollment program that allows high school students to work toward college degrees at community colleges. In 2009, nearly 19,000 students transferred from community colleges. Approximately 13 percent of these students were dual enrollment students, 31 percent went on to private four-year institutions and 56 percent transferred to public four-year institutions. Nearly half of the students graduating from a Washington college or university in 2006 took at least one class from a career or technical college. Transfer is common in Washington, as almost 40 percent of freshmen entering students and 70 percent of graduates had earned transfer credits.

The State has in place three transfer agreements that are being closely monitored to determine their impact. The Direct Transfer Agreement Associate degree (DTA), is focused on general education requirements; the Associate of Science-Transfer (AS-T), prepares students for biology, chemistry, earth science, physics, computer science, and engineering majors; and, the Major Related Programs (MRPs), prepares students for majors that require specific courses in the major, such as business and early childhood. The University of Washington provides transfer reports that show the breakdown of total credits by department earned by transfer and nontransfer students.[21] Generally speaking, transfer students earn more credits by graduation, but the margins do not appear to be large. New degree programs are showing potential for more parity.[22] Researchers conclude, "the bottom line is that transfer agreements help students graduate without excess credits, and transfer agreements in particular majors are especially helpful."[23]

The State of Florida has a much longer history of involvement in articulation and transfer. Starting in the 1970s, the state sought ways to decrease the time-to-degree for students. Florida uses a common course numbering system so that it is possible to determine equivalent courses across all public colleges and universities. Currently ten state universities, twenty-eight Florida Colleges (formerly community colleges), twenty-five participating non-public postsecondary institutions, and forty area technical education centers are part of the Statewide Course Numbering System. Florida is well known for its 2+2 system, which guarantees admission to a state college or university to students who complete their Associate degree. Although students are not guaranteed admission to the institution of their choice, they will enter with junior status. As a result, while the state's transfer rates are average as compared with the rest of the nation, their graduation rate is among the highest (48 percent for the 2006 cohort). Florida has also sought to make communication with students and school personnel a priority. The state's FACTS.org web site provides students with information about college, starting with information directed at middle school students. It also provides information on advising and counseling and all aspects of transfer.

SUCCESS STARTS AT THE COMMUNITY COLLEGE

While much attention has been directed to the role of baccalaureate institutions in transfer, community colleges also have a critical role to play. The manner in which community college counselors and advisors communicate with students shapes their transfer experiences. While some of the challenges with vertical relationships between institutions that have been described are known to researchers and policy makers, internal challenges at community colleges receive little attention. Internal processes and practices that need to be strengthened to increase the likelihood of baccalaureate attainment are readily apparent when seen though the lens of transfer.

The transfer process begins with transition into college. New community college students should be schooled in the transfer and articulation process at the time they enter college, rather than later in their community college careers. Since many community college students are first generation or immigrant students, they may not be able to obtain accurate and timely information about transfer from family and friends. Through orientation and student success courses, and even 100-level courses, students should be systematically introduced to four-year college options, including a thorough explanation of the types of courses that are known to articulate as well as those which do not. Emphasis needs to be placed on the importance of earning grades in the "A" and "B" range in general education courses as students risk having to retake courses in which they receive a grade of "C" or less if they choose to transfer.[24]

Simultaneously, students are better prepared for transfer when college standards are explicit. Publishing general education learning outcomes as well as course level outcomes will help students communicate with admissions officers at transfer institutions about their community college program of study. Currently, unless an articulation agreement is in place, discussion about curricula and courses needs to take place on a case-by-case basis. If community colleges demonstrate a commitment to standards and provide strong evidence relative to their assessment processes, transfer students will be in a much better position to make their case when transfer decisions come down to a case-by-case determination.

Student learning outcomes assessment efforts at community colleges must involve feedback from four-year institutions on the preparation of transfer students. The more information that community colleges can obtain about the outcomes of their transfer students, the better prepared they will be to leverage student success. The National Student Clearinghouse (NSC) provides data on institutions students transfer to, making it possible for researchers to follow students by exchanging data between institutional research offices. The example provided earlier of indicators used in in Washington State to track students is evidence of the usefulness of metrics as simple as the number of credits earned at the time of baccalaureate degree completion. Even if institutional research personnel do not have sufficient time and resources to devote to determining the number of courses that transferred and GPAs or other outcomes of their students at receiving institutions, they can employ electronic surveys with students to learn about transfer experiences. With some cooperation from four-year colleges, it may also be possible to communicate with transfer students by using their current college or university e-mail addresses, which should contribute to a higher response rate.

Community colleges are beginning to employ innovative methods for integrating their curricula with four-year institutions in order to support transfer success. Some community colleges have developed partnerships with four-year institutions that allow students to carry student IDs for both institutions. Holding a university ID makes it possible for students to use libraries and athletic facilities as well as attend events sponsored by four-year institutions.

Another approach involves partnering with four-year colleges and universities in offering baccalaureate degree programs on the community college campus. An excellent example of this is found at Macomb Community College in Michigan. The University Center at Macomb offers nearly fifty bachelor' and master's degree programs through nine university partners. More than 5,000 students are enrolled in these programs. In Massachusetts, high school students graduating with a GPA of 2.5 or higher can apply to a joint admission program which guarantees admission to the University of Massachusetts and most of the state's colleges. The Joint Admissions Program does not have blanket coverage across all majors and institutions, but many options are available to students.

Probably the trickiest area for transfer reform involves occupational degrees and certificates. For many community college students, courses taken toward a community college major are treated as elective credits at the four-year level. This can be a major setback for students in career programs, including business administration, education, nursing, communications, and criminal justice. Some states are empowering community college students by mandating statewide articulation agreement in career degree programs, including Washington and Texas. More often than not, however, the ability to articulate community college career-focused courses with those of a university remains problematic. For example, a national review of articulation agreements for students seeking degrees in education found only 15 statewide articulation agreements. [25]

In the end, community colleges may opt to solve the problem on their own grounds by establishing community college baccalaureate programs. It is no longer uncommon for community colleges to offer a small number of baccalaureate degrees, as the number of states providing community colleges with the ability to offer four-year degrees is growing. Typically, these degrees are in areas such as teaching, business, and nursing and the degree earned may be an applied baccalaureate. The growth of community college baccalaureate degrees is likely to continue, as they have been well received by students attending colleges offering them. Furthermore, the growth of these programs at community colleges is completely consistent with the historical development of higher education and with international trends. [26]

CONCLUSION

Variation in transfer rates, like variation in graduation rates nationwide, coupled with limited evidence of documented improvement in states that are actively involved in improving transfer, tell us that student success in transfer can be improved. The most difficult aspect may be getting a larger proportion of community college students to the point where they are academically ready for transfer. Students need to be provided with information about transfer and the articulation process early and continuously during their community college careers. For the substantial number of students starting in remediation, there is a question about the point at which to initiate discussion about transfer; however students who are interested in earning baccalaureate degrees need to *fully understand* how the system works at every contact point. Statewide articulation and core curricula can improve the reliability of information, as can electronic audit systems, which organize the complex network of articulation so that students can make informed choices.

NOTES

1.   John S. Levin et al., "The Recipe for Promising Practices in Community Colleges," *Community College Review* 38, no. 1 (2010).

2.   Clifford Adelman, "Answers in the Toolbox: Academic Intensity, Attendance Patterns, and Bachelor's Degree Attainment," (Washington, DC: U.S. Department of Education, 1999).

3.   Tatiana Melguizo, "Are Community Colleges an Alternative Path for Hispanic Students to Attain a Bachelor's Degree?," *Teachers College Record* 111, no. 1 (2009); ibid.

4.   Available   at   http://www.studentclearinghouse.org/about/pdfs/Clearing-house_profile.pdf.

5.   Adelman, "Answers in the Toolbox: Academic Intensity, Attendance Patterns, and Bachelor's Degree Attainment"; Alexander C. McCormick, "Swirling and Double-Dipping: New Patterns of Student Attendance and Their Implications for Higher Education," *New directions for Higher Education* 121(2003).

6.   Adelman, "Answers in the Toolbox: Academic Intensity, Attendance Patterns, and Bachelor's Degree Attainment," 41.

7.   Christine L. Sylvia, Shunyan Song, and Tony Waters, "Challenges in Calculating Two-Year College Student Transfer Rates to Four-Year Colleges," *Community College Journal of Research and Practice* 34(2010).

8.   Ibid., 571.

9.   Adelman, "Answers in the Toolbox: Academic Intensity, Attendance Patterns, and Bachelors Degree Attainment," 45.

10. U. S. Department of Education, National Center for Education Statistics, "Digest of Education Statistics," (Washington, DC: Author, 2010).

11. Demetra Kalogrides and Eric Grodsky, "Something to Fall Back On: Community Colleges as a Safety Net," *Social Forces* 89, no. 3 (2011), 869.

12. Barbara K. Townsend, "Redefining the Community College Transfer Mission," *Community College Review* 29, no. 2 (2001). Barbara K. Townsend and John T. Dever, "What Do We Know About Reverse Transfer Students?" New Directions for Community Colleges, 106 (1999).

13. Ellen M. Bradburn and David G. Hurst, "Community College Transfer Rates to 4-Year Institutions Using Alternative Definitions of Transfer," (Washington, DC: U. S. Department of Education, Office of Educational Research and Improvement, (June 2001), 22–23.

14. Peter Riley Bahr, "*Cooling out* in the Community College: What Is the Effect of Academic Advising on Students' Chances of Success?," *Research in Higher Education* 49(2008); W. Norton Grubb, "'Like, What Do I Do Now?': The Dilemmas of Guidance Counseling," in *Defending the Community College Equity Agenda*, ed. Thomas R. Bailey and Vanessa Smith Morest (Baltimore: Johns Hopkins University Press, 2006).

15. Burton R. Clark, "The 'Cooling out' Function Revisited," *New Directions for Community Colleges* 32, no. 1 (1980).

16. Clifford Adelman, "Moving into Town—and Moving On: The Community College in the Lives of Traditional-Age Students," (Washington, DC: U.S. Department of Education, February 2005); Sara Goldrick-Rab, "Following Their Every Move: An Investigation of Social-Class Differences in College Pathways," *Sociology of Education* 79, no. January (2006).

17. Goldrick-Rab, "Following Their Every Move: An Investigation of Social-Class Differences in College Pathways," 72.

18. Celia E. Rouse, "Democratization or Diversion? The Effect of Junior Colleges on Educational Attainment," *Journal of Business and Economic Statistics* 13(1995).

19. Tatiana Melguizo, Gregory S. Kienzl, and Marian Alfonso, "Comparing the Educational Attainment of Community College Transfer Students and Four-Year College Rising Juniors Using Propensity Score Matching Methods," *The Journal of Higher Education* 82, no. 3 (2011).

20. Carrie B. Kisker, Richard L. Wagoner, and Arthur M. Cohen, "An Analysis of Transfer Associate Degrees in Four States," (Los Angeles: Center for the Study of Community Colleges, April 2011).

21. Available at: http://www.washington.edu/admin/factbook/OisAcrobat/2010_timetod-eg_dept.pdf.

22. Washington Higher Education Coordinating Board, "Transfer Report," (March 2011), 12.

23. Ibid., 12.

24. Linda Serra Hagedorn, Jaime Lester, and Scott J. Cypers, "C Problem: Climb or Catastrophe," Community College Journal of Research and Practice 34, no. 3 (2010).

25. Jan M. Ignash and Ruth C. Slotnick, "The Specialized Associate's Degree in Teacher Education: Effective Pathway or Degree Proliferation?," *Community College Review* 35, no. 1 (2007).

26. Deborah L. Floyd and Kenneth P. Walker, "The Community College Baccalaureate: Putting the Pieces Together, " *Community College Journals of Research and Practice*, 33 (2009). Vanessa Smith Morest, "Double Vision: How the Attempt to Balance Multiple Missions Is Shaping the Future of Community Colleges" in *Defending the Community College Equity Agenda*, Thomas Bailey and Vanessa Smith Morest, Eds., (Baltimore: Johns Hopkins University Press, 2006). Debra Bragg and Collin Ruud, "Why Applied Baccalaureates Appeal to Working Adults: From National Results to Promising Practices, " *New Directions for Community Colleges*, 158, summer (2012).

Chapter Six

Organizational Change for Student Success

"Well, in our country," said Alice, still panting a little, "you'd generally get to somewhere else—if you run very fast for a long time, as we've been doing."

"A slow sort of country!" said the Queen. "Now, here, you see, it takes all the running you can do, to keep in the same place. If you want to get somewhere else, you must run at least twice as fast as that!"[1]

It may seem strange to start a chapter on educational reform with a quote from *Alice in Wonderland* but, like many community college leaders, the Queen is responsible for leading a world that is poorly understood by those coming from the outside. Implementing educational reform at community colleges can feel like running in quicksand because there are so many challenges to confront. As described throughout this book, community college students are generally at high risk of failure due to attributes beyond their control—low income, unsuccessful educational experiences in the past, being the first in their families to attend college, and so forth. Institutions also face major challenges, including shrinking budgets, a large part-time workforce, and bureaucratic constraints imposed by union contracts and centralized decision making. These realities coalesce to form a barrier to change that requires enormous effort to overcome. Just like Lewis Carroll's Queen, successful community college leaders must possess both a willingness to push the envelope, and the patience to persist in the face of resistance.

In the United States, efforts to reform public schooling are well documented as far back as the origins of compulsory education in the mid-1800s. Some of these efforts contributed to new paradigms of education, while others seem to have had little lasting impact.[2] Like Alice's experience in *Through the Looking Glass*, bringing about improvement in community college student success seems to require twice the effort imagined to be necessary. Why is real and lasting change so elusive? What do we know about organizational change that might make our efforts more efficient and fruitful?

ORGANIZATIONAL INERTIA

Community colleges are shaped by a landscape of influential forces that are external to daily operations. In organizational terms, environment is used to describe the external context and culture; politics and the economy contribute to the environment in which community colleges operate. The environment of public colleges and universities is described in organizational terms as complex. This is because public postsecondary institutions must be responsive to many different, and often conflicting, stakeholders. For leaders and staff working in a college, the result can be confusing and dysfunctional because so many interests are at stake. For example, a community college recently opened a beautiful new building financed through a state bond but was not given resources to cover security and cleaning of the new space because those funds are managed by a different state agency. Decision making in this sense appears to be irrational but may actually reflect the convergence of a series of independent decisions occurring in a loosely coupled system.

There are innumerable ways in which culture, politics, and the economy exert pressure on community colleges. The most obvious of these involves the political context. Community colleges are largely state entities, although states vary widely in the extent to which operations are centralized. In states such as New Jersey, community colleges are autonomous and there is minimal state infrastructure to support them, while other states, such as Virginia, maintain centralized systems. Among states with some degree of centralization, the extent to which policy decisions are centralized varies widely. One of the best indicators of how decision-making power is distributed in community college systems is the way in which boards of trustees are structured and who is responsible for appointing or electing trustees.[3] A locally elected board is likely to have different expectations of a president than a board appointed by the state. Beyond boards of trustees, there are elements making up the policy landscape of community colleges including funding mechanisms and collective bargaining entities that are influenced by political climate.

The economic context also generates external pressure including the distribution of resources to colleges from federal, state, and local sources, each of which has its own requirements that influence practice. For example, at a college on the Gulf Coast of Texas, Dow Chemical's political support is so important to the college that it has integrated credit and noncredit curricula to respond to the educational needs of Dow employees. While this would be an unusual structure at most community colleges, it makes sense at this institution and is accepted by college faculty and staff.

External pressures on community colleges emerging from local culture are highly influential. The status afforded the college and the role it plays in local and regional contexts impacts its approach to mission. Although the comprehensive community college has become the norm in most states and localities, community colleges vary widely in the relative emphasis placed on transfer and occupational programs.[4] For example, community colleges located near major public universities tend to have a strong orientation toward the transfer mission. Washtenaw Community College in Michigan, Blinn College in Texas, Santa Barbara City College in California, and Santa Fe College in Florida are examples. The role of community colleges in providing adult basic education and English as a Second Language is influenced by the distribution of responsibilities between high schools, community colleges, and other postsecondary providers. And the importance of the college itself as an employer can influence the way the institution is perceived and operates. Rural community colleges, for example, are often among the largest employers in their service areas, giving them a stronger position in local politics than institutions in urban areas.

These forces command the attention of community college leaders. Research on organizational dynamics has shown that the roles of administrators in public educational institutions have a bearing on how they manage impacts of the external environment on day-to-day educational activities.[5] An important role of college leaders is to maintain the stability of the organization in the face of rapidly changing conditions. This involves maintaining equilibrium for those directly involved in working with students to moderate the impact of external forces. Control is maintained through the organization's internal structure. For example, a hierarchy of authority guides committees, departments and responsibilities, and workload to ensure that people are working on the same page. In this way, change cannot occur outside of formal processes that are part of a chain of command. Stability is essential to organizational success in that it creates an environment in which students, policy makers, and employees invest time in the pursuit of a common goal. The downside of stability, however, is that the very structures supporting it can also create barriers to change, even when change is utterly necessary.

This is described as organizational inertia. Researchers studying organizations in the 1970s concluded that the effect of inertia on organizations was so great that significant change could only occur through the emergence of completely new and innovative organizations and the "death" of organizations that had become obsolete or unproductive. The hypothesis that innovation in an industry can lead to the birth and death of organizations may be applicable in the private sector, but it is not commonplace in educational organizations. In contrast, new organizational designs and innovations emerge side-by-side with existing structures and the organization becomes larger and more complex. In rare instances, new organizations are built from scratch. Cascadia College, in Washington State, opened in 2000; CyFair Community College, in the Lone Star College system on the outskirts of Houston, opened in 2003; and New Community College (enrolling students in fall 2012) in the City University of New York (CUNY) system are examples of colleges created for a specific purpose outside of the structure of existing institutions. These colleges were carefully planned to make student success the focal point of the organization. Innovative processes and systems were designed around student success, and instructors who valued collaborative teaching and learning as well as evidence-based practice were screened and selected.

Unfortunately for established colleges, the challenges that accompany organizational inertia are unavoidable. Inertia influences structures, policies, procedures, and systems that have become institutionalized in the culture of community colleges. The norms, beliefs, and values of college faculty and staff are deeply embedded thereby making change difficult, if not impossible to achieve. Long-serving faculty and staff were in place as colleges grew from a few classrooms to large, complicated, and diverse organizations. I once spoke with a president of a community college in Massachusetts who described teaching classes in the morning and helping to build walls to expand his college in the afternoon during the 1960s. At LaGuardia Community College in New York, President Gail Mellow described the college's initial cadre of faculty as believing that what they were doing was "fundamental to democracy" and that "the early faculty were young, and there hasn't been much turnover."[6] Pioneering instructors and staff have deep attachments to a college and can make or break efforts at organizational change.

WORKING AGAINST CHANGE

While the theoretical perspective I have just described would suggest that policy makers and leaders can do little to bring about organizational change, we know based on observation and experience that this is not entirely true. To some degree, this is a problem of definition as consensus is needed about what qualifies as organizational change. The development of initiatives aimed at improving the success rates of students may not meet the standard of organizational change if those initiatives are not institutionalized. From the perspective of leadership, bringing about large-scale structural and cultural organizational change is much more difficult than promoting smaller-scale interventions, although both can benefit students. Following are some examples of innovation requiring structural change.

Changing admissions and registration deadlines. Most community colleges continue to enroll students after classes begin. A shift toward earlier registration deadlines challenges traditional processes of community colleges, and the systemized belief that allowing students into classes up until the last possible moment maximizes access. At Valencia College in Florida, efforts to implement an earlier registration deadline resulted in the recognition that an earlier admissions deadline was also needed. The application deadline for Valencia is early August and registration ends one week later, so that these processes are complete for most students a full week before classes begin. Changing the registration deadline alone is simply changing a cutoff time, which could impede access. But shifting the process earlier became a cultural change which altered institutional norms. A clear message is sent to students that being admitted to college is a process that occurs no later than mid-summer, as opposed to late summer and fall.

Accelerating, integrating, and modularizing developmental education . Modular courses challenge the credit hour structure and the belief that developmental courses should parallel all other courses. Interventions in developmental skills showing promising results involve new ways of measuring progress and outcomes for students. Housatonic Community College, for example, is offering self-paced mathematics courses in which students proceed and advance as they are ready for next of level of work. The Community College of Baltimore County integrates remedial English students into college-level English through its Accelerated Learning Program. Initiatives of this type require faculty to work together in ways that cross departmental and disciplinary boundaries.

Making Pell grants available in the summer to boost student learning by supporting year-round education. The idea that students need time off during the summer is based largely on residential colleges. For commuting students, many of whom are part-time, summer downtime translates into a loss of momentum and a needless delay in completing classes. In 2010, the federal government began allowing students to obtain Pell grants to pay for tuition during the summer term. Although recent budget shortfalls have curtailed this practice, it represents a significant opportunity for students who need the summer term to maintain their academic momentum.

Developing and implementing learning communities and First Year Experience (FYE).

When organized as a First-Year Experience, learning communities represent significant organizational change. Rather than making them voluntary, learning communities can be mandated for all students in the first semester thereby encouraging them to attend full-time. This also challenges the norm of giving students unlimited choices when they first enter college. Research has shown that providing students with clear pathways and explicitly structuring their early college experiences can produce better results both short- and long-term. This is the premise upon which Completion by Design is built.

Using data and evaluation to guide decision making at community colleges. "Data driven decision-making" involves structural and cultural change. On the structural side, data systems must be developed and installed (often from scratch) to provide timely and accurate information. On the cultural side, application of data to governance, management, and instructional processes calls for normative change. The use of data and evaluation in pervasive ways challenges the belief that it is impossible to track data and that observation and experience provide the most accurate and unbiased information about student outcomes.

Bringing about structural and cultural change requires college-wide involvement and collaboration. In some instances, college personnel may need to assume new roles or responsibilities or alter the way they do their work. Regardless of the strategy, the institutionalization of large-scale change requires the redistribution of resources, both financial and human. Research on organizations in education and other sectors can provide insight into the challenges that come with organizational change, and levers that can remove barriers. In the next section, I review the characteristics of organizations that are important in bringing about large- scale change.

ORGANIZATIONS AND CHANGE

Researchers have theorized that change is slow and ineffective in public education because schools are loosely coupled structures and systems. The idea of coupling comes from the way in which train carriages are attached—or coupled—to one another with hooks. The "carriages" in higher education refer to the many categories we use to organize work. For example, colleges have broad categories of roles including administrators, staff, instructors, and students. Work is also organized around divisions (such as academic affairs and student services), departments, and programs. And time is structured in semesters, credit hours, evening, and day. In schools and colleges, couplings may correspond to one another, but not well enough for the carriages to be pulled in the same direction.

Evidence that organizational structures are loosely coupled abounds. How effective are communication channels among administrators, faculty, staff, and students? Those channels have to be intentional in order to be effective and include, newsletters, minutes, intranet, Internet, e-mail distribution lists, and so forth. How often do academic affairs and student affairs staff collaborate on projects? Colleges have made attempts at integrating these functions, but often encounter significant structural barriers. How many full-time instructors teach at night? The evidence suggests limited integration of the day and evening colleges. How often do departments hold meetings together? Knowing that community colleges are loosely-coupled organizations helps in the planning of organizational change because it encourages discussion about barriers to change.

Despite challenges to organizational change, there is ample evidence of instances in which innovation takes root at one college, and over time is widely adopted by many colleges. By studying how organizations develop and change in other fields, including the expansion of art museums and multi-national corporations, researchers have identified forms of external pressure that make organizations increasingly similar over time. They are defined as isomorphic tendencies of organizations and there are three different types of isomorphism: normative, coercive, and mimetic. [7]

Normative isomorphism refers to the tendency of institutions to respond to standards imposed by organizations assigned legitimacy. Accrediting bodies, for example, set standards, direct curriculum expectations, and encourage the development of an academic identity. Thus when curricula and support services and processes such as planning and governance in community colleges take similar forms it should come as no surprise that institutions, leaders, and staff develop similar views and outlooks regarding organizational development.

Coercive isomorphism stems from legislative and policy sources. Some of the most prominent examples of coercive isomorphism in postsecondary education are evidenced in the accountability mandates of government agencies: for example, structural changes associated with the development of data warehouses. States and colleges are finding that in order to keep up with the demands of accountability reporting, they can operate more efficiently with multidimensional databases. Over time, norms are shifting from limited data access through student information systems to the development of accessible data warehouses. The federal government became involved by encouraging database expansion through grant programs. The structure of colleges and state offices were impacted by the need to hire and train staff to develop and maintain data warehouses. Over time this changed the culture of colleges as the availability of large-scale descriptive data became the norm.

Although policy makers may not have anticipated that data warehouses would be developed in response to increased accountability requirements, colleges and state boards resonated with the idea after observing its success in early adopting colleges and states. This reflects a third category of change called *mimetic isomorphism* that occurs when mimicry results from information spreading through professional communication channels. For example, if one reviews annual conference programs for the past decade for associations such as the American Association of Community Colleges, the Association for Institutional Research, or the State Higher Education Executive Officers, one would see a progression toward common themes. Publications and other forms of communication between people working in the same area help to spread information about best practices, and over time institutions become increasingly similar in their structures and practices.

Another source of pressure bringing about organizational change is the dependence of organizations on resources.[8] Resources include financial resources, but also support from stakeholders. Using the example above, the availability of grant funds and state resources for the development and use of data systems contributes to increased interest in developing new systems. The association between funding and change can be seen the most clearly with respect to grant programs. For example, if the government wants to promote the development of health information technology certificate programs, change is encouraged by calling for requests for proposals that will lead to the establishment of new programs.

However, it is noteworthy that grant programs often do not appear to have the organizational impact envisioned by funders. For example, the results of an evaluation of the first five years of the Achieving the Dream initiative showed that many of the outcome indicators that funders and partners hoped would improve did not change: "despite college efforts to scale up their programs and services, the majority of strategies reached less than 10 percent of their intended target populations."[9] And, an evaluation of the National Science Foundation's Advanced Technological Education (ATE) program found little evidence that the initiatives funded were institutionalized.[10]

ADOPTION OF INNOVATION

Research on innovation diffusion has provided practical ways to think about how the process of organizational change can unfold and take root. Rogers[11] provides a model of innovation diffusion that can help colleges plan and prepare large-scale organizational change. Rogers's model of innovation diffusion, developed through research dating back to the 1940s, ranges across public and private industry sectors, which makes the theory robust in application. It is especially useful in educational organizations because of loose coupling.

Innovation diffusion on a college campus begins with the innovation-decision process which, according to Rogers, consists of five stages:

1. Knowledge: Formation of knowledge about the innovation.
2. Persuasion: Formation of an attitude toward the innovation.
3. Decision: The decision to adopt or reject the innovation.
4. Implementation: The implementation stage.

5. Confirmation: Confirmation of the decision to implement (or, alternatively, discontinuation

During the implementation stage, many innovations undergo reinvention. The concept of reinvention refers to "the degree to which an innovation is changed or modified by a user in the process of its adoption and implementation."[12] Most often, innovation does not occur through the replication of a particular change across colleges. Sometimes an innovation is too complex and must be simplified, or participants lack a full understanding of the innovation and adopt parts of it. Change can also be broad or abstract and implemented in a variety of ways depending upon context. Implementation always involves some form of interpretation and it is common for innovations to take different forms in different settings.

Personnel in a college that is implementing an innovation necessarily do not adopt the innovation at the same time. This may seem obvious, but understanding the dynamics of adoption can be helpful in planning successful change. Rogers identifies five categories of adopters. They are "normally" distributed. On a graph showing the number of adopters at various times in the adoption process, the result would be a bell curve, with a small number of innovators at one end, a small number of nonadopters at the other, and a large number of "majority adopters" in the middle. The five categories of adopters, in the order in which they would become involved in implementation, are as follows:

1. Innovators (2.5 percent)
2. Early adopters (13.5 percent)
3. Early majority adopters (34 percent)
4. Late majority adopters (34 percent)
5. Laggards (16 percent) [13]

Early majority adopters may be conflicted about the innovation, but are willing to take the risk; late majority adopters, originally skeptics, hold out until they are either convinced or presented with a lack of alternatives. The late majority adopters can be described as a resistant group who ultimately adopt change albeit reluctantly, while laggards avoid and ignore the change altogether to the greatest degree possible. The process of innovation adoption begins slowly and then accelerates once early majority adopters are on board. Of course, since adopters are cumulative, by the time the late majority adopters are transitioning to acceptance, adoption of the innovation is halfway complete. Research shows that this process unfolds reliably, but the speed of adoption varies. At community colleges, the speed of adoption can be influenced by unionization, inadequate financial resources, and the extent of support from leadership. [14] It can be sped up by the mimetic forces described in the previous section.

On community college campuses, we can easily spot innovators and early adopters. Innovators are those who pursue external funding, or are the "go to" people for college administrators. They are instructors who seek out grants and network with faculty outside their colleges to develop new ideas. Often they are informal leaders who recruit colleagues to work on projects with them. These individuals, in turn, become early adopters. It is in moving from early adoption to majority adoption that community colleges experience difficulty. An example is the difficulty encountered by developmental education initiatives in reaching the number of expected students. In an early account of the Developmental Education Initiative (DEI), researchers found that the initiative had fallen short of expectations because scaling up intervention was proving to be a slow and difficult process on campuses. Major obstacles included communication across departments and campuses, gaining buy-in, and hiring instructors and staff for key roles. [15]

What influences the rate of adoption, and how can an organization move from one phase to another as smoothly as possible? Network analysis documenting communication within organizations can be helpful in addressing adoption issues, as diffusion occurs through communication networks. Communication flows most freely between and among individuals who perceive themselves as having something in common. Network researchers use the concepts of homophily (sameness) and hetrophily (differentness) to capture this principle. In change, it is critical to have a communication plan in place. This is where college leadership can play a major role, by creating spaces in which consistent and positive communication can occur. Interdisciplinary and cross-functional teams can be helpful. Also, events or displays that allow faculty and staff to showcase their innovations can help to generate interest and understanding within a college. At a college with multiple unions, it may be necessary to work with each union because union communication channels can be particularly strong. A president of a Midwestern community college has union leaders represented on his president's council because it is conducive to generating college-wide buy-in to new initiatives

Bandwidth is also important to communication, and a simple rule of thumb prevails: where there are common interests and dispositions, bandwidth is greater. Since communication is essential to the adoption of innovation, adoption plans need to address how information will be disseminated. How will an understanding of shared interest and purpose develop as innovation moves toward acceptance? Decentralized decision making and loosely coupled departments are typical in community colleges, meaning that it is important to develop a sense of unity within a college in order for innovation to occur. The more faculty and staff perceive that they have something in common, the more easily information will flow through the institution. This is one of the reasons why meetings at which refreshments are served and interactive activities are offered provide opportunities to build a sense of camaraderie. The development of "core values" for the institution can similarly provide a foundation for strengthening communication channels as administrators, faculty, and staff formally acknowledge shared values.

Change agents—people who introduce an innovation and seek to develop a pool of innovators and early adopters—play a critical role. An individual may initiate change, but in order for adoption to occur, this person must successfully convince early adopters that change is necessary, worth the effort, and realistic within the given context. Success in the art of persuasion may be more elusive if a change agent is unable to develop trust relationships within the college. Unfortunately, administrators and faculty often do not work in harmony and do not display the kind of mutual respect that aids communication.[16] In number, administrators are the minority in colleges, so while they have the authority to attempt top-down change, true adoption cannot happen until faculty and staff have been convinced of the value of reform. The innovation being promoted can also play a role when external validation of the credibility of an innovation makes a convincing case to others.

POTENTIAL AND PITFALLS OF DISTRIBUTED LEADERSHIP

Experience with organizational change is beginning to provide insight into new ways of thinking about the role of college leaders. The Achieving the Dream literature presents a consistent message that leadership is critical to the success of reform.[17] Although all or most Achieving the Dream presidents would describe themselves as promoting student success and reform in their institutions, why do some institutions seem to move forward more quickly than others? One explanation may be that some institutions have been able to achieve buy-in on a much larger scale than others. Some of the best examples of buy-in are found among institutions that have earned awards over the past four years.[18] In 2012, for example, Zane State won an award on the basis of implementing a comprehensive advising system and encouraging first-year participation in remediation that increased remedial completion by more than 20 percent. Successful institutions are able to bridge an elusive threshold making reform an organic process and teamwork a way of doing business.

Recent research in K–12 schools and higher education is helping to develop an understanding of distributed leadership.[19] Distributed leadership challenges the perspective that leadership is a vertical process in which organizational change originates with individuals identified as serving in leadership positions.[20] The premise of the research on leadership is that meaningful distinctions exist between leaders and followers in a context that is change resistant and complex. For example, change may be initiated by faculty or staff unbeknownst to the formal leadership of an institution. In fact, the structure of higher education institutions may actually lend itself to distributed leadership because of the highly specialized knowledge sets of individuals serving in various roles.[21] The challenge for researchers studying community colleges and leaders working within them is to understand the role played by distributed leadership in shaping change and reform.

Distributed leadership can help or hinder progress toward improving student success, as faculty, staff, and administrators to whom others look for advice may not be in agreement about the direction the institution should take. In fact, some of the structural characteristics described earlier in this chapter, such as limited communication across departments and between categories of employees, contribute to difficultly in working toward common goals.

To bring about large-scale innovation, administrators must discern where leadership exists in the institution and nurture buy-in from those with leadership capacity. Sometimes this can be done by paying extra attention to "the meeting after the meeting." Participating in side conversations that occur as people leave meetings or striking up conversations with individuals who did not speak during meetings often provides practical information about how distributed leadership will affect plans for innovation and change.

TYING IT ALL TOGETHER

The obstacles that students face in achieving their academic goals are largely those that existed long before they entered the community college. They are tied to social class, educational background, and individual issues such as learning disabilities, academic or career anxieties, and limited English proficiency. Working against the odds to help students change the course of their lives is demanding work. Until recently, explorations into the efficacy of community college practice have been minimal, and community college faculty and staff have largely been left to figure it out on their own. This is no longer the case as more resources are being devoted to the problem and solutions are bound to emerge. Within the past decade, a wide range of reform efforts have been taking place on community college campuses nationwide. As of spring 2012, there were 167 participating and seventeen former Achieving the Dream colleges focusing on improving student success. Among them are fifty-two leader colleges which have been able to demonstrate three consecutive years of improvement on Achieving the Dream indicators.

But efforts at reform go well beyond these colleges because many are underway locally in systems and states seeking change. In 2007, the City University of New York (CUNY) launched the Accelerated Study in Associates Program (ASAP) which provides students with a rich array of supports and incentives for degree completion in three years, including comprehensive advising, tutoring, free textbooks and Metrocards in exchange for full-time enrollment and a commitment to graduate. The program has a goal of graduating 50 percent of its students within three years and early on is showing positive results in enrolling students full-time, credit earning, and retention.

Larger scale interventions are beginning to appear. Completion by Design is guided by the premise that graduation rates can be increased if students are given more precise pathways to follow and guidance and support throughout their college career. One of the first Completion by Design colleges, Miami Dade College in Florida, is initiating significant changes in remediation, advising, and curriculum that impact the entire institution. The State of Virginia is also undertaking large scale change through their Developmental Education Redesign. The redesign changes remedial placement and modularizes mathematics education across the entire community college system.

Community colleges are entering a new era—one of experimentation, innovation, and change. Three overlapping spheres are making these innovations possible. Researchers and funders comprise one sphere; practitioners at the college and system levels are the second; and the policy makers are the third sphere. The three spheres overlap, but their interests differ. Over the next decade we can expect to see coalescence among the spheres and an intensified focus on reform, particularly in the area of remedial education. Given the political landscape of these three interacting spheres, it will be important to keep the focus at all times on students and the impact of reform on access and success.

NOTES

1. Lewis Carroll, *Alice's Adventures in Wonderland, Through the Looking Glass* (New York: The Macmillan Company, 1897), 42.
2. David Tyack and Larry Cuban, *Tinkering toward Utopia: A Century of Public School Reform* (Boston: Harvard University Press, 1997).
3. Arthur M. Cohen and Florence B. Brawer, *The American Community College, Fourth Edition* (San Francisco: Jossey-Bass, 2003).
4. Thomas Bailey et al., "Educational Outcomes of Postsecondary Occupational Students," (New York: Community College Research Center, Teachers College, Columbia University, 2004).
5. John Meyer and Brian Rowan, "Institutionalized Organizations: Formal Structure as Myth and Ceremony," *American Journal of Sociology* 82, no. 2 (1977).
6. Betsy O. Barefoot and Michael J. Siegel, "Laguardia Community College: A Window on the World," in *Achieving and Sustaining Institutional Excellence for the First Year of College*, ed. Betsy O. Barefoot, et al. (San Francisco: Jossey-Bass, 2005), 61.

7. Paul J. DiMaggio and Walter W. Powell, "The Iron Cage Revisited: Institutional Isomophism and Collective Rationality," *American Sociological Review* 48(1983); Walter W. Powell and Paul J. DiMaggio, *The New Institutionalism in Organizational Analysis* (Chicago: University of Chicago Press, 1991).

8. Jeffrey Pfeffer and Gerald Salancik, *The External Control of Organizations: A Resource Dependency Perspective* (Palo Alto: Stanford University Press, 2003).

9. Elizabeth Zachry Rutschow et al., "Turning the Tide: Five Years of Achieving the Dream in Community Colleges," (New York: MDRC, 2011), 10.

10. Thomas R. Bailey et al., "Institutionalization and Sustainability of the National Science Foundation's Advanced Technological Education Program," (New York: Community College Research Center, 2003).

11. Everett M. Rogers, *Diffusion of Innovations, Fourth Edition*, 4th Edition ed. (New York: The Free Press, 1995).

12. Ibid., 174.

13. (Rogers, p. 262)

14. Rutschow et al., "Turning the Tide: Five Years of Achieving the Dream in Community Colleges."

15. Janet Quint et al., "Scaling up Is Hard to Do," (New York: MDRC, May 2011). Available online: http://www.mdrc.org/publications/595/full.pdf.

16. W. Norton Grubb, *Honored but Invisible: An inside Look at Teaching in Community Colleges* (New York: Routledge, 1999).

17. Carol Lincoln, "Courageous Conversations: Achieving the Dream and the Importance of Student Success," *Change Magazine*, no. January/February (2009).

18. Two major awards are the Leah Meyer Austin Award (see http://www.achievingthedream.org/people/leah-meyer-austin) and the Aspen Prize for Community College Excellence (see http://www.apseninstitute.org/policy-work/aspen-prize/about).

19. James P. Spillane, *Distributed Leadership* (San Francisco: Jossey-Bass, 2006).

20. Jitse D. J. van Ameijde, Patrick C. Nelson, and Jon Billsberry, "Improving Leadership in Higher Education Institutions: A Distributed Perspective," *Higher Education* 58(2009).

21. Richard Bolden, Georgy Petrov, and Jonathan Gosling, "Tensions in Higher Education Leadership: Towards a Multi-Level Model of Leadership Practice," *Higher Education Quarterly* 62, no. 4 (2008).

Chapter Seven

Moving the Needle on Student Success

Community college students possess multiple risk factors which work against their odds of completion or transfer. While scholars debate whether community college students would be more successful if they began their postsecondary careers at four-year colleges and universities, it is reasonable to conclude that the 50 percent of community college students who are at greatest risk would have limited success in either type of institution.

Throughout this book the challenge of improving student success at community colleges has been explored from multiple perspectives. Basically the difficulties faced by students can be viewed as falling into three buckets. First, the academic preparation bucket. Standard community college assessment practices indicate that the majority of community college students do not demonstrate college level mathematics and English skills at entry. The second bucket is the social bucket. For many students, the strong social connections on campus that would enable them to become integrated into the academic community of college are lacking. The third bucket is financial. Many community college students are paying for college themselves, which means their financial situation—including financial literacy and financial decision making—may affect persistence and completion. The interventions chosen to address these buckets approximate where change can occur. Unfortunately, too many community college students face challenges in all three areas, so while an intervention might plug a hole in one bucket, the other two continue to leak.

Research has provided some important insights into student success at community colleges. Synthesizing the more detailed findings described throughout the book into manageable bites can help leaders and staff create interventions that enhance student success.

THE ACADEMIC BUCKET

The academic challenges faced by community college students are well documented. The reality is that the students with the greatest academic needs are directed to the postsecondary institutions with the least resources in the public sector. Public four-year institutions spent $36,000 per FTE in 2009–2010, whereas public two-year colleges spent $12,000.[1]

Problems with the weak academic preparation of students have been present throughout the history of community colleges.[2] Remedial education, intended to address this problem, is not effective for most students. This has been confirmed for many years by quantitative analyses across all higher education sectors. Analyses conducted by Attewell et al. cite Adelman's decade-old observation that, based on his analyses of students attending college in the 1980s and 1990s: "'remediation' in higher education is not some monolithic plague that can be cured by a single prescription. Determined students and faculty can overcome at least mild deficiencies in preparation . . . . But when reading is the core of the problem, the odds of success in college environments are so low that other approaches are called for."[3] Current community college practice, however, places a cohort of twenty to thirty academically low-performing students in classrooms for several hours a week with the assumption that they can succeed over a period of time. Standard approaches that rely on placement testing followed by remedial education if necessary are under intense scrutiny. Different pedagogical approaches are being tested with a goal of providing intervention alternatives to improve the outcomes of remediation.

Socioeconomic status (SES) is known to play a critical role in student success. SES is a strong predictor of academic preparation. Racial and ethnic minorities are more likely to begin college in remediation. Differences in academic preparation reflect, in large part, gaps in the quality of K–12 schools, even for those students who have been out of high school for several years. SES also correlates with the likelihood of being the first in one's family to attend college. When combined with other characteristics, SES makes it difficult to become integrated into the college community. And while the aspiration of the open door college has been to provide access, and by so doing, provide hard-working students with the opportunity to overcome their socioeconomic circumstances, the reality is that current practice at community colleges is inadequate to help them overcome the barriers to their potential.

Community college students are challenged by circumstances that predate their arrival on campus. Some can be related to variability in the performance of K–12 schools. The composition of school districts often concentrates low SES students in particular schools on the basis of geography. Curriculum and teaching in low SES schools are rarely adequate to improve the outcomes of low SES students. Further, there may be lower expectations in terms of curriculum requirements with fewer mathematics and English courses that students must complete during high school, compounding skills that are already marginal. Many students treat their senior year lightly, taking low-demand courses that contribute to marginal performance on placement tests, leading in turn to a higher risk of failure in college. It is hoped that the common core curriculum will bring about improvement in these areas. Learning disabilities, anxieties about subject areas such as mathematics, writing, or reading, and difficulties stemming from English language proficiency add to students' learning challenges.

Although interventions over the past decade have resulted in improvement, in truth, community colleges have a limited number of power tools in the toolbox. Remediation, in its current form with semester-long courses in sequences of two to three semesters, clearly does not work for many students. Focusing on K–12 to college transitions may offer some hope for improving student outcomes. In this respect, community colleges are at an advantage in comparison to four-year colleges and universities that work with much larger service areas. The students who are likely to attend community colleges are known long before college matriculation. While interventions at the high school level can be costly and result in expansion of the community college mission, becoming more deeply involved in K–12 education is increasingly being viewed as a necessity for community colleges.

THE SOCIAL BUCKET

Well-meaning efforts to ensure access work against basic social science knowledge about how retention in higher education works. First-year students need to have opportunities to forge connections with faculty and peers on campus even when commuting from home. It is also important for institutions to communicate with their students in a systematic way during the first semester to prepare them for participation in a culture of success. The most direct way to ensure that this happens is through structures such as learning communities and student success courses where curricula can be used to encourage and develop social and academic integration into the college community.

In general, community colleges are not well positioned to provide social supports to students because they operate on relatively small budgets. While community colleges spend approximately 9 percent of their per FTE expenditures on student services, this is $337 *less* per FTE than public four-year colleges (about 25 percent).[4] Practices that limit interaction between students and college faculty and staff include high student to counselor ratios, high ratios of students to advisors, collective bargaining agreements that govern faculty advisory roles and limit office hours, and the prevalence of part-time faculty.

The social challenges experienced by community college students can be described in terms of cultural capital. The theory of cultural capital, developed by sociologist Pierre Bourdieu,[5] has been applied to many educational settings, including the work of Annette Lareau in elementary school classrooms.[6] In her research, Lareau observed that low SES parents interact with schools and teachers very differently than high SES parents. As part of her study, parents were observed at "open house" nights. Lareau noted that, "many of the [low SES] parents did not speak with a teacher during the visit. When they did, the interaction tended to be short, rather formal, and serious."[7] In interviews, these parents "expressed doubts about their educational capabilities and indicated that they depended on the teacher to educate their children."[8] By contrast, open house nights at the high SES school in her study were attended by 96 percent of parents (compared with 60 percent at the low SES school) and "almost all of the parents talked to a teacher or to the teacher's aide; these conversations were often long and punctuated by jokes and questions."[9] High SES parents approached teachers as equals and partners in educating their children—they engaged them as opposed to deferring to them.

These differences in behavior had important educational consequences for children in Lareau's study. She concluded that social class influences schooling as high SES parents were culturally better aligned with their children's teachers and understood each other. This was not true of lower SES parents, who minimized their interactions with teachers as a way to diffuse their discomfort. An individual's cultural capital consists of an accumulation of his or her past experience.

What can be drawn from the theory of cultural capital is that community college students may lack the cultural capital to succeed in college. Community college faculty and staff are highly educated and have embraced and internalized the culture of academe. Students, on the other hand, may have less of a basis for this kind of cultural alignment. Many are likely to have been raised by parents similar to those described by Lareau; those who avoided conversation with teachers, focused mainly on nonacademic issues, and kept to the periphery of classrooms. Students displaying similar behaviors might be interpreted by faculty as hostile toward school or disinterested in education.

At the beginning of their postsecondary careers, many community college students are strangers to the culture of college and are unclear about college-level expectations. They lack an "intuitive" understanding of how to interact with faculty and staff and frustrate and disappoint faculty with what appears to be an absence of motivation, disinterest in academic subjects, and poor study skills. Attention to cultural alignment between students and the college environment will need to be better understood if community colleges are to help students achieve academic and career goals.

THE FINANCIAL BUCKET

Students choose community colleges because they are proximate and affordable. The incentive structure that shapes college choice results in community colleges enrolling a disproportionate number of students who do not have adequate resources to pay for college and who are overwhelmed by time and financial commitments. Because two-thirds of students enroll part time, it can take years to complete a community college education, during which time burdens of family and work commitments can overwhelm students.

While tuition at community colleges remains relatively low, many students are financially independent and contribute to family finances. Moreover, job demands often interfere with college success. As a result, a number of risk factors correlate with low income, including part-time attendance, full-time work while in college, and stop-out. Performance-based scholarships have shown some promise for improving outcomes. Higher levels of support that could alleviate financial barriers is a desirable solution, but one that is too costly, and therefore not feasible for most colleges.

Supports that might help students address financial challenges are more likely to be programmatic than monetary. Educational practices such as internships and service learning can help students network within their communities, which can lead to paid employment. Additionally, strengthened connections with community organizations can also provide support for students. Community-based organizations (CBOs) can be useful partners for community colleges because they are structured and funded to provide social services in ways that community colleges are not. It may be possible to engage or forge agreements that place social workers on campus. There are also CBOs that specialize in financial literacy and provide access to electronic systems that inform students of public benefits for which they qualify. These types of services can help relieve external pressures in students' lives so that they can focus on succeeding in college.

LEADING THE WAY TO STUDENT SUCCESS

College practitioners engaged in improving student success know that significant reform is needed in order to achieve change. This is certainly not a reflection of the level of commitment and professionalism typically found at community colleges. The problem is significant because too many students attending community colleges face challenges to persistence and completion rooted in academic, social, and financial problems. Community colleges have evolved around a deeply held value of access to education. Many of the structures associated with ensuring access—last minute deadlines for decisions related to registration and withdrawal and remedial placement policies—are now proving to be barriers to improving student success.

To begin thinking about the prospects of cultural change, it is useful to step back and consider how community colleges look in comparison to K–12 schools, which have long been under intense public scrutiny. K–12 schools have decades of experience with ongoing efforts at reform. Is this the fate of community colleges? The answer is probably "no," because community colleges have several characteristics that differentiate them from K–12 schools. First, there are fewer of them, while states looking to reform K–12 schools are dealing with hundreds of schools. Community colleges number just over 1,000 nationwide and most states have fewer than twenty. Second, community colleges are, by comparison, a tightly knit sector. There are numerous venues for information exchange across colleges, including national conventions, regional meetings, and nationwide initiatives such as Achieving the Dream. It is perhaps this collegiality that has contributed to a third asset, which is the ability of community colleges to attract resources to support their reform initiatives in the form of grants that supplement state funding.

Achieving scale on an institutional level will be more difficult than achieving scale on a systemic level. Bringing reform to scale on an institutional level—or disruptive innovation—involves cultural change. A useful distinction can be made between the "technologies" of reform and the "culture" of reform. Throughout this book I have mentioned the technologies of reform—strategies and innovations such as learning communities, modularized curricula, and statewide articulation agreements. Identifying the technologies of reform involves creativity, trial and error, and evaluation. Replicating and broadening the impact of successful technologies involves culture, and this is where community colleges need to focus their attention. Well-known management expert Peter Drucker observes that "culture eats strategy for breakfast." At community colleges, culture sometimes nibbles and sometimes devours the technologies of reform, but it rarely stays out of the way. Three areas of culture are particularly important to reform efforts: accountability; curricula and teaching; and working in networked organizational structures.

Focus on Accountability

In our personal lives, we use the ability to measure and quantify results to our advantage. The simplest example involves measures of health. Every visit to a physician begins with measuring weight and blood pressure. These measures do not tell us all that much, for it is difficult to interpret a small change—is it a trend or an anomaly? Furthermore, we know that both measures are arrayed on a bell curve, and therefore to some degree the differences between individuals are meaningless. We use these measures primarily because they are easy and inexpensive, and changes in level correlate with underlying problems requiring further examination. In truth, there are ways to measure aspects of weight and blood pressure that can provide more insight, but they require specialized tools and specialists who are trained to use them. Overall, the benefits of using imperfect measures such as weight and blood pressure outweigh the costs.

There are lessons that can be taken from these simple procedures measuring physical health. First, they are only descriptive tools. They are not analytical, and do not provide explanation for observed change. They are subject to inaccuracy based on context—for example, the equipment being used or specific events surrounding the time of measurement. If we want to know what is really going on, we use different, more robust measurement techniques that can morph into a wide range of explanations from food choice to psychology. Similarly, many of the measures that we use to determine the health of a community college do not give us any helpful insights. IPEDS (Integrated Postsecondary Educational Data System) graduation rates, for example, have come under much scrutiny because they do not measure important aspects of community college service. In their current form, IPEDS graduation and transfer rates leave out the two-thirds of students who are not full-time and are distorted by the fact that two-thirds of the students being measured are not starting at college-level when the time clock for measurement begins. They also do not take into consideration factors that would affect outcomes, such as the demographic characteristics of students.[10]

There are important differences when comparing measures of health against those used to measure student success. The purpose of keeping track of body weight and blood pressure reflect a private concern with monitoring health. On the other hand, accountability has been framed by policy makers as a public concern for improving institutional performance. In other words, underlying accountability is the belief that the public is entitled to transparency and evidence of productivity. From an institutional perspective, it may be more helpful to think about accountability measures as ways to monitor the health of a college. What is needed are clearly stated standards and simple, inexpensive ways to monitor organizational health so that goals can be set for improvement, and leaders can easily gauge institutional performance.

Community colleges need not and should not rely on external forces to drive monitoring strategies. Our colleges have become increasingly adept at measuring performance and have made this part of standard business practice. Taking the analogy a step further, if you want to change your weight, take a baseline measurement and set a goal. If you are serious about reaching the goal, buy a scale and weigh yourself at regular intervals. Community colleges are taking measurements and setting goals. The problem is that we know all too well that, while food intake and exercise are levers to bring about a change in weight, levers relating to the outcomes of community college students are less well known and considerably less direct.

Montgomery County Community College in Pennsylvania is a college that has worked extensively with metrics to monitor organizational health. Under the leadership of its president, Karen Stout, Montgomery developed a balanced scorecard to measure and report college-wide performance. Conceptually, balanced scorecard measures are somewhat like baseball statistics that bring indicators such as productivity in pitching, hitting, and errors together in a table. Arrows pointing up and down indicate the direction that the most recent measurement took in relation to past measurements. It is also possible to set goal ranges; for example, a course completion rate of 0–65 percent could be red, 66–75 percent could be orange, and 76 percent or higher could be green. This allows for an immediate snapshot of where the college is relative to a wide range of goals.[11]

Throughout this book I have provided descriptions of data sources being used by community colleges and policy makers to understand quality and productivity. These data sources are also part of a system for monitoring the health of institutions. There are other methodologies for accountability, in addition to the balanced scorecard, such as benchmarking, which can be conducted using institutional historical data or data comparison with peer institutions.

Most of the national surveys provide benchmarking as a routine function, to enable colleges to determine where they are relative to other institutions. There are many contextual variables shaping community college outputs—a circumstance that makes accurate benchmarking comparisons difficult. College size, demographic profile (race, ethnicity, and age distributions), balance of full- and part-time students, and the proportion of students receiving Pell grants are all measures that must be taken into account in benchmarking. Additionally, community colleges are heavily influenced by state policy, making comparisons across states difficult. Measures of student engagement may be called into question because they are self-reported, but measures such as transfers, workforce development, financing, and organizational structures (e.g., class size and developmental education requirements) tend to be more accurately compared because they are transparent.

One of the best examples of community college benchmarking is the National Community College Benchmarking Project (NCCBP), which is directed by Jeff Seybert at Johnson County Community College (Kansas). In 2011, the NCCBP processed and reported data from 280 participating community colleges across the nation. Participating colleges pay a subscription fee and submit data to a database which allows them to harvest information on how they compare to similar institutions submitting data to NCCBP. The benchmarking data are organized into three categories: Students and Student Outcomes, Institutional Effectiveness, and Community and Workforce Development.

A critical first step in transforming community colleges to become success focused is to develop methods of tracking student outcomes that are simple and efficient. Institutional size is an important determinant of the practicality of developing such a system as scale is critical to making the process efficient. Monitoring provides only rudimentary information, however, and it must be done as efficiently as possible in order to be effective. Going back to the analogy of weight and blood pressure, imagine a world in which these two measurements required hours of human labor, sophisticated knowledge or expensive tools. There would be inequality in our ability to monitor health, for those without resources would not be able to afford the cost of the service. Further, taking these measurements might actually undermine health because they would drain resources away from the very activities that could lead to better health, such as joining a fitness club or buying healthy food. Similarly, small institutions, and those for which the costs of obtaining data are high because of inefficient data systems, are at a significant disadvantage.

Measuring progress toward student success must become internally focused if it is to become part of the process of improving outcomes. The measures that policy makers are looking for in accountability mandates are not the same measures that will provide meaningful feedback internally regarding progress toward improved outcomes. Therefore, part of the solution to improving student success must involve integration and alignment of the goals of policy makers, college administrators, and faculty, and staff. Measurements that offer a big picture of performance through comparison across institutions and time need to be developed and maintained. Internally, researchers can play a critical role as institutional leaders and participants on interdisciplinary teams that are working toward generating the information needed to address persistent problems in student success. Furthermore, adopting the practices of computer adaptive testing and student learning outcomes assessment will make it far easier and more efficient for faculty to concentrate on the areas where students need to improve.

Renewed Focus on Curriculum and Pedagogy

Since the best predictor of success in community college courses is past academic performance, it follows that a major focus of reform efforts needs to be on the classroom. Community college students differ from four-year college students in important ways—they are commuting to campus, older on average, juggling multiple responsibilities, and have struggled academically in the past. Teaching community college students is a specialized task, and methods of working successfully with this population need to be developed and shared.

A number of teaching techniques have proven to be helpful with community college students. Collaborative and hands-on pedagogies engage students in classroom activities. Wherever possible, using applied curricula and contextualized learning can help to reduce the anxiety students experience when learning abstract concepts. The idea of heterogeneous classrooms in which students of different academic levels are combined has proven successful in K–12 schools, and early results from the Accelerated Learning Program at the Community College of Baltimore County show promise for community college students as well. Learning communities offer a variety of benefits including reduction of student workload by combining assignments. In addition, contextualized learning and culturally aware teaching methodologies deserve attention at community colleges to help faculty and students improve their understanding of each other.

Transfer is an area of student success in which alignment of goals at all levels of the system is critical. States have sought to support community colleges in this area through policies involving curriculum, including developing a statewide core curriculum and leveling courses to increase consistency across institutions. In some states, policies provide incentives for students, for example mandating that students who complete their associate degrees be admitted as juniors to four-year colleges and universities, or supporting concurrent admissions to the community college and a public university. And there are statewide supports for articulation involving electronic course auditing systems that provide students with information about which universities in the state will accept courses they have taken. All of these programs reinforce the curriculum at the community college level as a conduit to enrollment and completion at baccalaureate degree institutions.

Student learning outcomes have an important role to play. Curriculum mapping and establishing standards allow for important communication among faculty. Making standards available to students brings them into the curriculum so they can understand the connection between topics and courses. Assessment of student outcomes provides detailed information on curricular gaps and weaknesses as well as strengths. It can help diagnose why students are failing and provide a roadmap for prioritizing curriculum development.

Degree pathways and clearly articulated systems help students succeed. Practices that are moving community colleges in this direction include educational planning systems, such as Valencia Community College's Life Map,[12] in which early on students engage in career exploration and goal setting. Since many community college students are the first in their families to attend college, they do not have family members who can help in solving problems or making critical connections on campus. Building supports for students into systems of advising and counseling are important. Classroom practices such as defining and measuring student learning outcomes can also help by making the community college curriculum more transparent to students. The use of e-portfolios can help by enabling students to make connections and develop independence as learners. Clearly defined pathways can reinforce and tighten connections between systems as well, so that transitions between levels of education (K–12, community colleges, and baccalaureate institutions) are seamless.

Networking Knowledge with Experience

Experience with community college reform is demonstrating that there is strength in both numbers and diversity. The Achieving the Dream initiative evolved out of a partnership among eight organizations, each of which brought expertise such as research, publicity, leadership, and educational reform to the table. Months of debate and discussion produced the foundation underlying Achieving the Dream. Today, the faculty and staff at ATD colleges have opportunities to connect with one another through webinars, the Internet, and the annual DREAM Institute. In 2012, the DREAM Institute was attended by more than 1,500 community college faculty, staff, and administrators as well as researchers, foundations, and advocates who could share ideas and information about student success across state and institutional boundaries.

Similarly, the Carnegie Foundation for the Advancement of Teaching's Statway and Quantway initiatives rely on teams. In this initiative, the team involves researchers, curriculum experts, faculty, and institutional researchers from pilot institutions. This model gives credence to the process of knowledge development through collaboration. It does not assume that the answers are known, but that institutions have the capacity to find them through shared expertise.

These efforts have in common an approach to change that is simultaneously top-down and bottom-up. Rather than relying on existing networks that reinforce the status quo, these initiatives engage leaders and staff in networks that are organized around student success. Understanding that leadership is distributed, rather than hierarchical, means that leaders must re-conceptualize their work. In a flattened organization, they become team members working shoulder to shoulder with others. Their task is to identify and amplify the positive results of instructors and staff who are working directly with students. Students understand the experience of being a learner best, and should not be overlooked as potential team members along with community stakeholders and business and industry representatives.

PROMISE OF THE FUTURE

In 1995, Deborah Meier published The Power of Their Ideas which was about an experiment with small schools in Harlem.[13] Her ideas and insights were gained through service as principal of this school, where she was able to create a culture of success. Students at Meier's school, regardless of background or academic potential, were lifted to success by a school that refused to let them down. Meier's leadership philosophy is based on the conviction that every student can succeed:

> The task of creating environments where all kids can experience the power of their ideas requires unsettling not only our accepted organization of schooling and our unspoken and unacknowledged agreement about the purposes of schools. Taking this task seriously also means calling into question our definitions of intelligence and the ways in which we judge each other. And taking it seriously means accepting public responsibility for the shared future of the next generation.[14]

The climate surrounding community colleges today is not all that different from the one in which Meier's Central Park East Secondary School flourished. Community colleges are under increasing public scrutiny regarding the success of their students. There is also an erosion of public support in the form of state financing, although political support remains strong. One could say that the major difference between K–12 schools and community colleges is that students are mandated to attend K–12 schools, but have choice when it comes to community colleges. Students vote with their feet, however, and many acknowledge that college no longer seems voluntary because a degree or certificate is required for most reasonably compensated jobs.

As the title of this book suggests, multiple stakeholders need to be involved in achieving a culture of success. Policy makers, funders, advocates, administrators, staff, faculty, and students must all focus on common goals. Aside from placing greater value on graduation and reinforcing this through systems and pathways to guide students, colleges need to value the individual student. Our colleges face major challenges in this area, as students spend very little time on campus. Not only are students likely to be part time, so are instructors. From the perspective of evening students, the college administration and staff are practically nonexistent. If students are to achieve success, an investment must be made in counteracting obstacles. Community building that encourages students to form bonds with each other and with faculty and staff, is important to success. Emphasizing teamwork and opportunities to get to know peers during classroom time and as part of the curriculum can help this happen. Learning communities, student success courses, and service learning opportunities are practices that provide instructors with opportunities to help students become connected to the college community.

Finally, although much has been learned over the past decade about success at community college there is still much research and evaluation to be done. Community college leaders and staff need to understand what is working on their campuses. Which instructors and staff are effective, and what can they teach us about working with students? Which students are effective, and what are the secrets of their success? Open and engaged discussion and debate will contribute to the development of critical insights in every corner of our colleges.

NOTES

1. NCES, "Digest of Education Statistics," (Washington, DC: National Center for Education Statistics, 2011), Table 377. For a more complete understanding of expenditure differences between sectors, please see the Delta Cost Project (http://www.deltacostproject.org/analysis/index.asp).

2. Arthur M. Cohen and Florence B. Brawer, *The American Community College, Fifth Edition* (San Francisco: Jossey-Bass, 2009).

3. Clifford Adelman, "The Toolbox Revisited: Paths to Degree Completion from High School through College," (Washington, DC: U.S. Department of Education, 2006); Paul Attewell, Scott Heil, and Liza Reisel, "Competing Explanations of Undergraduate Noncompletion," *American Educationl Research Journal* 48, no. 3 (2011), 11.

4. NCES, "Digest of Education Statistics," Table 373.

5. Pierre Bourdieu, "Cultural Reproduction and Social Reproduction," in *Power and Ideology in Education*, ed. Jerome Karabel and A. H. Halsey (New York: Oxford University Press, 1977).

6. Annette Lareau, "Social Class and Family-School Relationships: The Importance of Cultural Capital," *Sociology of Education* 69, no. April (1987).

7. Ibid., 78.

8. Ibid., 79.

9. Ibid., 78.

10. The final report of the Committee on Measures of Student Success may be retrieved at http://www2.ed.gov/about/bdscomm/list/cmss-committee-report-final.pdf.

11. For a more thorough discussion of indicators, please see Richard L. Alfred et al., *Core Indicators of Effectivness for Community Colleges*, Edition 2, (Washington, DC: Community College Press, 1999).

12. Sanford C. Shugart and Joyce C. Romano, "Focus on the Front Door of the College," *New Directions for Community Colleges*, no. 144 (2008).

13. Deborah Meier, The Power of Their Ideas: Lessons for America from a Small School in Harlem, (Boston, MA: Beacon Press, 2002).

14. Ibid, 4.

Index

About the Author

Vanessa Smith Morest is Dean of Institutional Effectiveness at Norwalk Community College. She is an adjunct assistant professor of Higher and Postsecondary Education at Teachers College, Columbia University, and an affiliate of the Community College Research Center. Dr. Morest holds a Doctorate in Sociology of Education from Teachers College, Columbia University. Prior to her current position, she served as Assistant Director for Postsecondary Research at the Community College Research Center, Teachers College, Columbia University (CCRC). Morest has more than twelve years of experience conducting research on community colleges concerning a wide range of topics. Her research has focused on community college organization, leadership, and policy. Morest is co-editor of *Defending the Community College Equity Agenda* (2006). She is past president of the National Council for Community College Research and Planning and has participated on numerous committees and initiatives related to increasing the success of community college students.